Samuel Waddington

The Sonnets of Europe

A Volume of Translations

Samuel Waddington

The Sonnets of Europe
A Volume of Translations

ISBN/EAN: 9783337228507

Printed in Europe, USA, Canada, Australia, Japan

Cover: Foto ©ninafisch / pixelio.de

More available books at **www.hansebooks.com**

THE

SONNETS OF EUROPE

A VOLUME OF TRANSLATIONS

Selected and Arranged, with Notes,

BY

SAMUEL WADDINGTON.

'*Laborum dulce lenimen.*'—HOR.

LONDON:
Walter Scott, 24 Warwick Lane, Paternoster Row,
AND NEWCASTLE-ON-TYNE.
1886.

TO

MY FRIEND

AUSTIN DOBSON.

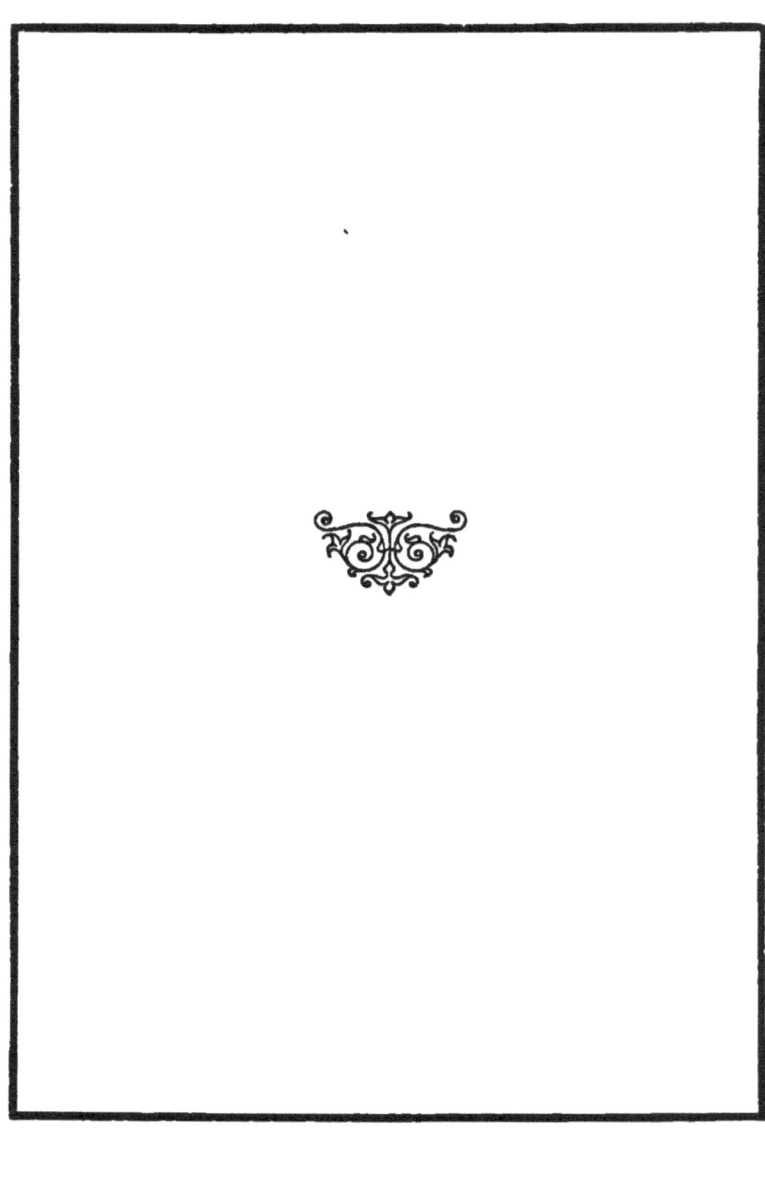

AUTHORS AND TITLES.

An asterisk is prefixed to those Sonnets which have not been previously published.

ITALIAN SONNETS.

		PAGE
FRA GUITTONE D'AREZZO—		
Love's Bondman . .	*Henry Francis Cary*	1
GUIDO GUINICELLI—		
Of His Lady . . .	*Henry Francis Cary*	2
GUIDO CAVALCANTI—		
To Dante . . .	*Percy Bysshe Shelley*	3
Love and Lapo . .	*Warburton Pike*	4
Whatso is Fair . .	*Henry Francis Cary*	5
BONAGGIUNTA URBISANI—	.	
Wounded of Love . .	*Charles Bagot Cayley*	6

AUTHORS AND TITLES.

		PAGE
DANTE ALIGHIERI—		
To Guido Cavalcanti	*Percy Bysshe Shelley*	7
To Brunetto Latini	*Henry Francis Cary*	8
On the 9th June 1290	*Henry Francis Cary*	9
Love's Messenger	*Warburton Pike*	10
From the "Vita Nuova"	*Sir Theodore Martin*	11
From the "Vita Nuova"	*Sir Theodore Martin*	12
From the "Vita Nuova"	*Sir Theodore Martin*	13
From the "Vita Nuova"	*Thomas W. Parsons*	14
From the "Vita Nuova"	*Charles Eliot Norton*	15
From the "Vita Nuova"	*Charles Eliot Norton*	16
From the "Vita Nuova"	*Henry Francis Cary*	17
From the "Vita Nuova"	*Henry Francis Cary*	18
From the "Vita Nuova"	*James Russell Lowell*	19
CINO DA PISTOIA—		
Why Sighest Thou?	*Warburton Pike*	20
FOLGORE DA SAN GEMIGNANO—		
On Knighthood (I.)	*John Addington Symonds*	21
" " (II.)	*John Addington Symonds*	22
FRANCESCO PETRARCA—		
Love's Fidelity	*Earl of Surrey*	23
Love's Inconsistency	*Sir Thomas Wyatt*	24
She Ruled in Beauty	*Thomas W. Higginson*	25
Doth any Maiden Seek	*Thomas W. Higginson*	26
Those Eyes, 'neath which	*Thomas W. Higginson*	27
Dreams Bore my Fancy	*Thomas W. Higginson*	28
Oft by my Faithful Mirror	*Thomas W. Higginson*	29
Gentle Severity	*Thomas W. Higginson*	30
The Buried Heart	*Barbarina, Lady Dacre*	31
Love's Pilgrimage	*Barbarina, Lady Dacre*	32
Visions of Laura	*Thomas Russell*	33
A Stolen Glove	*Charles Bagot Cayley*	34
Two Roses	*Charles Bagot Cayley*	35
The Heart on the Hill	*Charles Bagot Cayley*	36
Signs of Love	*Charles Bagot Cayley*	37
Quitting Vaucluse	*Charles Bagot Cayley*	38
On the Projected Crusade	*Charles Bagot Cayley*	39
GIOVANNI BOCCACCIO—		
On Dante	*F. C. Gray*	40

AUTHORS AND TITLES.

		PAGE
LORENZO DE' MEDICI—		
Violets	*William Roscoe*	41
Seek he who will	*William Roscoe*	42
In Tears	*William Roscoe*	43
LEONARDO DA VINCI—		
*Of Will, Power, and Duty	*Samuel Waddington*	44
JACOPO SANAZZARO—		
Mors Et Vita	*James Glassford*	45
MICHAEL ANGELO—		
The Transfiguration of Beauty	*J. Addington Symonds*	46
Thanks for a Gift	*J. Addington Symonds*	47
The Garland and the Girdle	*J. Addington Symonds*	48
The Doom of Beauty	*J. Addington Symonds*	49
Celestial Love	*J. Addington Symonds*	50
Love, the Light-Giver	*J. Addington Symonds*	51
Love's Entreaty	*J. Addington Symonds*	52
On the Brink of Death	*J. Addington Symonds*	53
A Prayer for Purification	*J. Addington Symonds*	54
Love's Justification	*William Wordsworth*	55
To the Supreme Being	*William Wordsworth*	56
LODOVICO ARIOSTO—		
In Will's Despite	*James Glassford*	57
PIETRO BEMBO—		
" Ye Haunts Recluse "	*James Glassford*	58
The Dream	*James Glassford*	59
VITTORIA COLONNA—		
The Massacre of the Innocents	*James Glassford*	60
" Ye are the Branches"	*James Glassford*	61
FRANCESCO COPPETTA—		
In Dreamland	*James Glassford*	62
CLAUDIO TOLOMEI—		
The Evening Star	*Anon*	63

AUTHORS AND TITLES.

		PAGE
BERNARDO TASSO—		
The Fountain	*James Glassford*	64
GIOVANNI DELLA CASA—		
To Sleep	*J. Addington Symonds*	65
ERASMI DI VALVASONE—		
Mormoranti Famosi	*James Glassford*	66
TORQUATO TASSO—		
To Ferrante	*James Glassford*	67
Love	*J. Herman Merivale*	68
Love Unloved	*James Glassford*	69
*To a Mature Beauty	*Baroness von Gilsa*	70
Oft Have we Heard	*John Hoole*	71
GIOV. BATTISTA MARINI—		
*Lux Umbra Dei	*Baroness Von Gilsa*	72
In Memoriam	*James Glassford*	73
GABRIELLO CHIABRERA—		
The Italian People	*Sir Aubrey de Vere*	74
GIORDANO BRUNO—		
The Philosophic Flight	*J. Addington Symonds*	75
TOMMASO CAMPANELLA—		
The World's a Stage	*J. Addington Symonds*	76
The Human Comedy	*J. Addington Symonds*	77
The People	*J. Addington Symonds*	78
To Ridolfo Di Bina	*J. Addington Symonds*	79
The Book of Nature	*J. Addington Symonds*	80
The Modern Cupid	*J. Addington Symonds*	81
The True Kings	*J. Addington Symonds*	82
The Resurrection	*J. Addington Symonds*	83
SALVATOR ROSA—		
*———	*William Michael Rossetti*	84

AUTHORS AND TITLES.

		PAGE
PETROCCHI—		
I Call on Time	*James Glassford*	85
GIULIO BUSSI—		
Of Glory	*Sir Aubrey de Vere*	86
LODOVICO PATERNO—		
Ye Airs! Sweet Airs	*Henry Francis Cary*	87
FRANCESCO REDI—		
The Garden of Earthly Love	*Edmund Gosse*	88
The Creation of My Lady	*Edmund Gosse*	89
Grief	*Edmund Gosse*	90
Love, the Musician	*Edmund Gosse*	91
The End of Earthly Love	*Edmund Gosse*	92
VINCENZO DA FILICAJA—		
Of Providence	*Leigh Hunt*	93
Where, Italy, 's Thine Arm	*Thomas Le Mesurier*	94
Buried Cities	*Thomas Le Mesurier*	95
No, not to Thee	*James Glassford*	96
To Italy	*Anon*	97
GIOVAM. CRESCIMBENI—		
I Ask the Sky	*James Glassford*	98
G. COTTA—		
Love's Canticle	*James Glassford*	99
GAETANA PASSERINI—		
Genova Mia	*James Glassford*	100
ZAPPI—		
As toward the Ascrean Mount	*Thomas Le Mesurier*	101
The Statue of Moses	*Sir Aubrey De Vere*	102
PIETRO METASTASIO—		
O Fair Unsullied Rose	*James Glassford*	103
FAUSTINA MARATTI—		
The Rival	*Thomas Russell*	104

CLEMENTI BONDI—		PAGE
A Husband's Homily	*James Glassford*	105
CASTI—		
The Debt of the *Giuli Tre*	*Leigh Hunt*	106
,, ,, (IL.)	*Leigh Hunt*	107
PASTORINI—		
To Genoa	*Leigh Hunt*	108
VITTORELLI—		
On a Nun	*Lord Byron*	109
BETTINELLI—		
Venice	*James Montgomery*	110
GABRIELE ROSSETTI—		
*Status Quo	*William Michael Rossetti*	111

FRENCH SONNETS.

MELLIN DE SAINT-GELAIS—		
*The Sonnet of the Mountain	*Austin Dobson*	115
PIERRE RONSARD—		
Voici Le Bois	*Robert, Earl of Lytton*	116
Page, Suy Moy	*Robert, Earl of Lytton*	117
Two Flowers I Love	*Henry Francis Cary*	118
*Avant qu' Amour	*Cosmo Monkhouse*	119
Roses	*Andrew Lang*	120
Of His Lady's Old Age	*Andrew Lang*	121
*Another Rendering	*C. Kegan Paul*	122
On His Lady's Waking	*Andrew Lang*	123
His Lady's Death	*Andrew Lang*	124
His Lady's Tomb	*Andrew Lang*	125
*The Apparition	*Thomas Ashe*	126
*On His Astræa's Arising	*Thomas Ashe*	127

AUTHORS AND TITLES.

		PAGE
JOACHIM DU BELLAY—		
It Was the Time, When Rest	Edmund Spenser	128
On High Hill's Top I Saw	Edmund Spenser	129
*Happy the Man	Austin Dobson	130
*Regrets	Austin Dobson	131
To Heavenly Beauty	Andrew Lang	132
To His Friend in Elysium	Andrew Lang	133
JACQUES TAHUREAU—		
Shadows of His Lady	Andrew Lang	134
Moonlight	Andrew Lang	135
LOUISE LABE—		
*Long as I Still	Arthur Platt	136
ESTIENNE JODELLE—		
The Ivy, Holly, and Green Bay	Henry Francis Cary	137
AMADIS JAMYN—		
A Game at Football	Henry Francis Cary	138
PHILIPPE DESPORTES—		
An Invitation	Henry Francis Cary	139
*The Fugitive	Samuel Waddington	140
THÉOPHILE DE VIAU—		
Sleep	Edmund Gosse	141
PAUL SCARRON—		
The Black Doublet	R. H.	142
MOLIÈRE—		
*To M. la Mothe le Vayer	Austin Dobson	143
FELIX ARVERS—		
*The Secret	Thomas Ashe	144
Another Rendering	Henry Wadsworth Longfellow	145
ALBERT GLATIGNY—		
Before the Snow	Andrew Lang	146

AUTHORS AND TITLES.

J. TRUFFIER—
    PAGE
    The Burial of Molière . . . *Andrew Lang* 147

BAUDELAIRE—
    The Day's End . . . *Arthur Reed Ropes* 148
    Meditation . . . *Arthur Reed Ropes* 149
    *The Rebel . . . *Cosmo Monkhouse* 150

SULLY PRUDHOMME—
    The Shadow . . *Arthur O'Shaughnessy* 151
    Profanation . . *Arthur O'Shaughnessy* 152
    The Struggle . . *Arthur O'Shaughnessy* 153
    The Appointment . *Arthur O'Shaughnessy* 154

GERMAN SONNETS.

G. A. BÜRGER—
    The Heart without a Home . . *Capel Lofft* 157

J. WOLFGANG VON GOETHE—
    The Maiden Speaks . . . *E. A. Bowring* 158
    To a Golden Heart . . *Margaret Fuller Ossoli* 159

C. AUGUST TIEDGE—
    In Memoriam (Theo. Körner) . *Charles T. Brooks* 160

THEODORE KÖRNER—
    Queen Louisa . . . *Charles T. Brooks* 164

L. A. VON CHAMISSO—
    Last Sonnet . . . . *Anon* 165

J. W. LUDWIG GLEIM—
    Cynthia Bathing . *Thomas Russell* 166

AUTHORS AND TITLES.

A. G. Von Platen-Hallermünde—   PAGE
   Fair as the Day . . . . *Anon* 167

J. Ludwig Uhland—
   *The Death-Angel . . . *M. Dickson* 168
   The Two Maidens . . . *Alexander Platt* 169
   The Conversion to the Sonnet . *Alexander Platt* 170

Heinrich Heine—
   *Fresco Sonnets to Christian S—— . *M. Dickson* 171
        "   " . *Stratheir* 172
   *To My Mother . . . *M. Dickson* 173
        "   " . *Stratheir* 174
   Fain Would I Weep . . . *E. A. Bowring* 175

SPANISH SONNETS.

   Had I a Thousand Souls . . *Sir J. Bowring* 179

Tome Burguillos—
   To-morrow and To-morrow . . *Sir J. Bowring* 180

M. Vazquez De Leca—
   To Leander . . . . *Sir J. Bowring* 181

Francisco De Figueroa—
   The Death of G. de la Vega . *Hon. William Herbert* 182

Santa Teresa De Avila—
   'Tis not Thy terrors, Lord . . *Sir J. Bowring* 183

Francisco Quevedo—
   Rome . . . . . *Felicia Hemans* 184

Juan De Tarsis—
   Thou, who hast fled . . *Felicia Hemans* 185

AUTHORS AND TITLES.

MIG. DE CERVANTES—   PAGE

The Author to His Pen	*J. Y. Gibson*	186
From Don Quixote	*Charles Jarvis*	187
" "	*Charles Jarvis*	188
Last Sonnet	*J. Y. Gibson*	189

LOPEZ MALDONADO—

The Brook	*Henry Wadsworth Longfellow*	190

LOPE DE VEGA—

To-Morrow	*Henry Wadsworth Longfellow*	191
The Good Shepherd	*Henry Wadsworth Longfellow*	192
La Vida es Sueno	*C. Tomlinson*	193
Not Winter Crystal	*Lord Holland*	194
Sonnet on the Sonnet	*J. Y. Gibson*	195

LUPERCIO LEONARDO—

Truth and Beauty	*J. Y. Gibson*	196

P. CALDERON DE LA BARCA—

*These Flowers whose pomp	*Arthur Platt*	197

PORTUGUESE SONNETS.

LUIS DE CAMOENS—

An Adieu to Tagus	*J. J. Aubertin*	201
The Death of King Sebastian	*J. J. Aubertin*	202
To a Fillet	*J. J. Aubertin*	203
Sibella	*J. J. Aubertin*	204
If Thou Indifference	*J. J. Aubertin*	205
Corydon and Tityrus	*J. J. Aubertin*	206
The Fisher Ionio	*J. J. Aubertin*	207
The Shepherdess Nise	*J. J. Aubertin*	208
Audaces Fortuna Juvat	*J. J. Aubertin*	209
Catharina De Athaide	*J. J. Aubertin*	210
On the Death of C. De Athaide	*J. J. Aubertin*	211
The Eyes Where Love	*J. J. Aubertin*	212
Beholding Her	*Robert Southey*	213
His Insufficiency of Praise	*Richard Garnett*	214

AUTHORS AND TITLES.

		PAGE
J. XAVIER DE MATOS—		
Night-fall	Richard Garnett	215
RODRIGUEZ LOBO—		
Past Joys	Richard Garnett	216
FRANCISCO DE ALDANA—		
The Native Land	Henry Wadsworth Longfellow	217
The Image of God	Henry Wadsworth Longfellow	218
CURVO SEMEDO—		
It is a Fearful Night	William Cullen Bryant	219
MANOEL DU BOCCAGE—		
*On Nelson	J. J. Aubertin	220

SWEDISH SONNETS.

GUSTAV ROOSENHANE—		
*Deep in a Vale	Edmund Gosse	223
*And There I Sat Me Down	Edmund Gosse	224
OLOF WEXIONIUS—		
*The Death of a Lady	Edmund Gosse	225
STAGNELIUS—		
*Hope Repulsed	Edmund Gosse	225
*Luna	Edmund Gosse	227
*Memory	Edmund Gosse	228

POLISH SONNETS.

MICKIEWICZ—		
The Rock of Aiudah	Richard Garnett	231
Eastward, the Sun	Richard Garnett	232

GREEK SONNETS.

ARISTOMENÊS PROVILEGIOS— PAGE
    Ah, now at last . . *E. Mayhew Edmonds* 235

ALEX. R. RHANGABE—
    *Love . . . . *E. Mayhew Edmonds* 236

DUTCH SONNETS.

P. CORNELISZOON HOOFT—
    *To Hugo Grotius . . . *Edmund Gosse* 239
    *Friendship . . . . *Edmund Gosse* 240

JAN VAN BROEKHUIZEN—
    Beyond the Rhine . . . *Sir J. Bowring* 241

LATIN SONNET.

HUGO GROTIUS—
    *To Thomas Farnable . . *Samuel Waddington* 242

NOTES 245

Preface.

HE sonnets of Dante and Michael Angelo, of Petrarch, Camoens, and Ronsard, could hardly fail to attract even those who are not especially interested in this form of verse—while to those who are, it were difficult to imagine what would furnish greater delight than the perusal of the works of these "old masters" of the "sonnet." But the large majority of readers may not be able to study these compositions in the various languages in which they were originally written, and they must consequently have recourse to such translations as may be found scattered through the pages of our own poets. These, moreover, are contained in numberless volumes, many of which may not always be readily accessible, and it is therefore hoped that a fairly representative selection of these

translations may prove of service, and a source of pleasure, to those who wish to become acquainted with the gems, modern or antique, of foreign poesy.

Many of the sonnets, translations of which are included in this volume, were composed more than three hundred years before Milton wrote his *Paradise Lost* — some of them more than two hundred years before the birth of Shakespeare— yet they are, for the most part, as fresh as flowers newly gathered, and possessed of a grace and delicate fragrance that have outlived the passing of so many centuries. But while a large number of the original sonnets are of this ancient date, the greater portion of the translations, as, for instance, those by Mr. Aubertin, Mr. John Addington Symonds, and Mr. Andrew Lang, have been written during recent years, and many of them are here published for the first time. Of those previously unpublished, mention may be made of Mr. Gosse's rendering of the Swedish and Dutch sonnets; Mr. William Michael Rossetti's translations of sonnets by Salvator Rosa and his father, Gabriele Rossetti; Mr. Thomas Ashe's translations from the French; Mr. Arthur Platt's from Louise Labé, Calderon, and Lope de Vega; Mrs. Edmond's from the modern Greek

PREFACE.

poets; those by Dr. Richard Garnett from the Portuguese; by Mr. Cosmo Monkhouse from Ronsard and Baudelaire; by the Baroness von Gilsa from Tasso and Marini; and the very able rendering of Boccage's fine sonnet "On Nelson," by Mr. J. J. Aubertin, to which we would call special attention.

The translation of a sonnet from one language into another in the legitimate, or Italian, sonnet-form is attended with some difficulty; and it is to this difficulty of translation that we are probably indebted for what is now known as the English, or Shakespearian, form of the sonnet. It was first used by the Earl of Surrey, who translated several of Petrarch's sonnets, and also composed a few original poems, in this form, which is much easier for the purposes of translation than that in which the Italian poets wrote. The following is an example of the latter, and is, moreover, the oldest sonnet extant in any language, it having been written by Piero delle Vigne about the year 1220 A.D.

NATURA D' AMORE.

Però ch' Amore non si può vedere,
E non si tratta corporalemente,
Manti ne son di si folle sapére
Che credono ch' Amore sia niente !

> Ma poi ch' Amore si face sentère
>   Dentro del cor signoreggiar la gente,
> Molto maggiore pregio de' avere
>   Che se 'l vedesse visibilemente.
> Per la virtute della calamita
>   Como lo ferro attrae non si vede,
> Ma si lo tira signorevolmente.
> E questa cosa à credere m' invita
>   Che Amore sia, e dammi grande fede
> Che tuttor sia creduto fra la Gente.

It will be seen that the rhymes in the octave of the above are alternate, and a large number of the early Italian or Petrarchan sonnets follow this arrangement of the rhymes. At page 23 of this selection will be found a translation of one of Petrarch's sonnets by Surrey in which the rhymes are alternate, but the translator has apparently been compelled to adopt fresh rhymes in the second quatrain in order to be able to more closely follow the sense of the original poem. Now this use of additional rhymes in the second quatrain constitutes the main difference between the Italian and the Shakespearian form of the sonnet, for if the rhymes were the same as those used in the first quatrain, the sonnet would then be a legitimate Italian sonnet. As regards the use of the final couplet, it should be mentioned that although rare, it is to be found in the early Italian sonnets, and a few of those by Petrarch have this termination. The majority of modern critics agree that the final couplet detracts from the beauty of the composition, but they also agree that the following (all of which close with a final couplet) are amongst the best of our English sonnets:— Blanco White's "Night and Death," Keats's "Last Sonnet," Michael Drayton's "Last Chance," Sir Philip Sidney's "With how sad steps, O moon,—" Wordsworth's "Sonnet on the Sonnet," Mrs. Fanny Kemble's "Art thou already weary of the way," Leigh Hunt's "Nile," Tennyson-Turner's "Time and Twilight," Hartley Coleridge's "Long time a child, and still a child, when years,—" Cowper's "To Mary Unwin," Donne's "To Death," Rossetti's "Match with the Moon," Matthew Arnold's Sonnet on "Shakespeare," etc.

But to return to the subject of this volume, the domain of translation, it may be observed, extends from the most bald and literal substitution of word for word, and line for line, on the one hand, to mere paraphrase, interpretation, or imitation, on the other,—and Lord Woodhouselee, in his interesting Essay on the Principles of Translation, published at the close of the last century, points out that neither of these extremes can be deemed satisfactory. It is, however, to D. G. Rossetti that

xxiv   *PREFACE.*

we are indebted for the most intelligent and comprehensive criticism on this subject. "The life-blood," he writes, "of rhythmical translation is this commandment,—that a good poem shall not be turned into a bad one. The only true motive for putting poetry into a fresh language must be to endow a fresh nation, as far as possible, with one more possession of beauty. Poetry not being an exact science, literality of rendering is altogether secondary to this chief law. I say literality,—not fidelity, which is by no means the same thing. When literality can be combined with what is thus the primary condition of success, the translator is fortunate, and must strive his utmost to unite them; when such object can only be attained by paraphrase, that is the only path."

A good poem shall not be turned into a bad one. How far the compositions in the present volume comply with this great commandment of rhythmical translation must be left to the reader to determine, but the editor has endeavoured, however unsuccessfully, to adopt it as his κανών καὶ μέτρον in making this selection. Bramston, the worthy and witty Vicar of Starting, wrote more than a century ago—

"True taste to me is by this touchstone known,
That's always best that's nearest to my own,"—

yet an editor may indeed esteem himself fortunate who finds that the consensus of public opinion confirms his own judgment.

It only remains for me to thank Mr. J. A. Symonds, Mr. Edmund Gosse, Dr. Garnett, and others, for much valuable assistance generously accorded,—as well as those holders of copyright who have given me permission to include various sonnets in this volume.

SAMUEL WADDINGTON.

47 Connaught Street, Hyde Park,
November 1886.

Italian Sonnets.

AUGUST GRAF VON PLATEN-HALLERMÜNDE.

TO SCHELLING.

With a Volume of Poems.

Is he not also Beauty's sceptre bearing,
   Who holds in Truth's domain the kingly right?
   Thou seëst in the Highest both unite,
   Like long-lost melodies together pairing.
Thou wilt not scorn the dainty, motley band,
   With clang of foreign music hither faring,
   A little gift for thee from Morning-land,—
   Thou wilt discern the beauty they are wearing.
Among the flowers, forsooth, of distant valleys,
   I hover like the butterfly, that clings
   To summer-sweets and with a trifle dallies:—
But thou dost dip thy holy, honeyed wings,
   Beyond the margin of the world's flower-chalice,
   Deep, deep into the mystery of things.

                                       Anon.

ITALIAN SONNETS.

FRA GUITTONE D'AREZZO.

Love's Bondman.

GREAT joy it were to me to join the throng
   That thy celestial throne, O Lord, surround,
   Where perfect peace and pardon shall be found,
   Peace for good doings, pardon for the wrong;
Great joy to hear the vault of heaven prolong
   That everlasting trumpet's mighty sound,
   That shall to each award their final bound,
   Wailing to these, to those the blissful song.
All this, dear Lord, were welcome to my soul,
   For on his brow then every one shall bear
   Inscribed, what late was hidden in the heart;
And round my forehead wreath'd a lettered scroll
   Shall in this tenor my sad fate declare:
   "Love's bondman, I from him might never part."

Henry Francis Cary.

GUIDO GUINICELLI.

OF HIS LADY.

I would from truth my lady's praise supply,
   Resembling her to lily and to rose;
   Brighter than morning's lucid star she shows,
   And fair as that which fairest is on high.
To the blue wave, I liken her, and sky,
   All colour that with pink and crimson glows,
   Gold, silver, and rich stones: nay, lovelier grows
   E'en love itself, when she is standing by.
She passeth on so gracious and so mild,
   One's pride is quenched, and one, if sick, is well :
   And they believe, who from the faith did err ;
And none may near her come by harm defiled:
   A mightier virtue have I yet to tell ;
   No man may think of evil seeing her.

                    Henry Francis Cary.

GUIDO CAVALCANTI.

To Dante.

Returning from its daily quest, my Spirit
   Changed thoughts and vile in thee doth weep
      to find:
It grieves me that thy mild and gentle mind
Those ample virtues which it did inherit,
Has lost. Once thou didst loathe the multitude
   Of blind and madding men: I then loved thee—
I loved thy lofty songs, and that sweet mood
   When thou wert faithful to thyself and me.
I dare not now, through thy degraded state,
   Own the delight thy strains inspire—in vain
I seek what once thou wert—we cannot meet
   As we were wont. Again and yet again
Ponder my words: so the false Spirit shall fly,
   And leave to thee thy true integrity.

                    Percy Bysshe Shelley.

GUIDO CAVALCANTI.

Love and Lapo.

If you, my Dante (*this I pray
   You much*), see Love with Lapo near,
   Take heed, and then if Love you hear
   Call Lapo lover, write and say ;—
And tell me, if his lady's sway
   Seem kind, and he in guise appear
   Of gallant, since such folk, I fear,
   When tired of work, at loving play !
You know, when in his court Love reigns
   No one can serve, but he who's true,
   A lady who is wandering there ;—
And if his patience favour gains,
   The marks of that are known to you,
   Your style, and mine, the emblems bear.

Warburton Pike.

GUIDO CAVALCANTI.

Beltà di donna e di saccente core.

Whatso is fair in lady's face or mind,
   And gentle knights caparison'd and gay;
   The singing of sweet birds to love inclined,
   And gallant barks that cut the watery way;
The white snow falling without any wind,
   The cloudless sky at break of early day,
   The crystal stream, with flowers the meadow lined,
   Silver, and gold, and azure for array:—
To him that sees the beauty and the worth
   Whose power doth meet and in my lady dwell,
   All seem as vile, their price and lustre gone;
And, as the heaven is higher than the earth,
   So she in knowledge doth each one excel,
   Not slow to good in nature like her own.

Henry Francis Cary.

BONAGGIUNTA.

Wounded of Love.

Wounded, I pray my wounder to beware
   Lest me, by plucking out her barb, she slay;
For many dying I have seen, that were
   Not killed by wound, but weapon drawn away.
For this I will my wound in quiet bear,
   And live with patience, if but live I may;
For all he conquers, who will not despair;
   A man by patience wins in every fray.
I ask then of thy mercy, O my light,
   Sweet lady, and my solace all alone,
   Withdraw not from my deadly wound thy spear;
Choose not, for God's love, I should perish quite;
   My sorrow's port I hope to find anon;
My heart has learnt not by long pain to veer.

Charles Bagot Cayley.

DANTE ALIGHIERI.

To Guido Cavalcanti.

Guido, I would that Lapo, thou, and I,
    Led by some strong enchantment, might ascend
    A magic ship, whose charmèd sails should fly
    With winds at will, where'er our thoughts might wend,
And that no change, nor any evil chance,
    Should mar our joyous voyage; but it might be
    That even satiety should still enhance
    Between our hearts their strict community,
And that the bounteous wizard then would place
    Vanna and Bice and my gentle love,
    Companions of our wandering, and would grace
With passionate talk, wherever we might rove,
    Our time, and each were as content and free
    As I believe that thou and I should be.

                    Percy Bysshe Shelley.

DANTE ALIGHIERI.

To Brunetto Latini.
(Sent with the *Vita Nuova*.)

Master Brunetto, this I send entreating
   Ye'll entertain this lass of mine at Easter;
   She does not come among you as a feaster;
   No: she has need of reading, not of eating.
Nor let her find you at some merry meeting,
   Laughing amidst buffoons and drollers, lest her
   Wise sentence should escape a noisy jester;
   She must be wooed, and is well worth the weeting.
If in this sort you fail to make her out,
   You have amongst you many sapient men,
   All famous as was Albert of Cologne.
I have been posed amid that learned rout,
   And if they cannot spell her right, why then
   Call Master Giano, and the deed is done.

Henry Francis Cary.

DANTE ALIGHIERI.

ON THE 9TH JUNE 1290.

CAME Melancholy to my side one day,
   And said, "I must a little bide with thee;"
   And brought along with her in company
   Sorrow and Wrath.   Quoth I to her, "Away:
I will have none of you: make no delay."
   And, like a Greek, she gave me stout reply.
   Then, as she talked, I looked and did espy
   Where Love was coming onward on the way.
A garment new of cloth of black he had,
   And on his head a hat of mourning wore:
   And he, of truth, unfeignedly was crying.
Forthwith I asked: "What ails thee, caitiff lad?"
   And he rejoined: "Sad thoughts and anguish sore,
   Sweet brother mine! our lady lies a-dying."

Henry Francis Cary.

DANTE ALIGHIERI.

Love's Messenger.

A TENDER thought comes oft to me,
    Of you to whisper, and remain,
    And sings of love, so sweet a strain
    My heart, entranced, must needs agree.
Says Soul to Heart, *Pray, who is he,*
    That cometh to console our pain,
    And so o'erpowering makes his reign,
    Scarce other thought in us can be?
The answer this,—*Soul, full of thought,*
    He comes from Love a spriteling new,
    Who his desires to me hath brought;
His life and forces all, he drew
    From Her, the loving one, who knows,
    And sees with pitying eyes, our woes.

                      Warburton Pike.

DANTE ALIGHIERI.

From the "Vita Nuova."

Riding some days agone in piteous mood,
    Heart sick and weary with the journey's fret,
    Full in the middle of the way I met
Love in a pilgrim's habit, worn and rude.
His air, methought, was sadden'd and subdued,
    As he had been despoilèd of his sway;
    And he came, sadly sighing, up the way,
With downcast eyes, unwilling to be view'd.
When he beheld me, calling me by name,
    I come, he said, *from yon far region, now,*
    Where dwelt thy heart, while that to me seem'd fit,
And for new service back am bringing it.
    Then I so wrapt in thought of him became,
    That he had vanished, and I know not how.

                          Sir Theodore Martin.

DANTE ALIGHIERI.

From the "Vita Nuova."

Love hath his throne within my lady's eyes,
    Whence all she looks on wears his gracious mien.
    All turn to gaze, when she abroad is seen,
    And whom she greets from him his colour flies;
With downward gaze he stands abashed, and sighs,
    Remembering all his own unworthy blames.
    Anger and pride before her fly. Ye Dames,
    Lend me your aid her matchless worth to prize!
All gentleness, all thoughts serene and meek,
    Grow in the heart of him that hears her voice.
    To see her once is ever to rejoice;
Her look, when a faint smile is on her cheek,
    Nor tongue can tell, nor memory hold in view,
    So winning-gracious is the sight, and new.

Sir Theodore Martin.

DANTE ALIGHIERI.

From the "Vita Nuova."

Art thou the man, who hast so often sung
   To us the worth that in our lady lies?
   Thy voice is his full surely, but thy guise
Proclaims thee of a different lineage sprung.
Why dost thou weep, with heart so sorely wrung,
   That others look on thee with pitying eyes?
   Say, hast thou seen her weep, and in such wise,
Thou could'st not hide the grief that to thee clung?
Leave us to weep, and sadly range along.
   He doth a sin who seeks to comfort us;
   For we have heard her in her anguish cry;
And so deject her look, and piteous,
   That whosoe'er should view such sorrow's wrong,
   Must feel his heart for grief within him die.

Sir Theodore Martin.

DANTE ALIGHIERI.

From the "Vita Nuova."

So gentle seems my lady and so pure
When she greets any one, that scarce the eye
Such modesty and brightness can endure,
And the tongue, trembling, falters in reply.

She never heeds, when people praise her worth,—
Some in their speech, and many with a pen,
But meekly moves, as if sent down to earth
To show another miracle to men !

And such a pleasure from her presence grows
On him who gazeth, while she passeth by,—
A sense of sweetness that no mortal knows
Who hath not felt it,—that the soul's repose
Is woke to worship, and a spirit flows
Forth from her face that seems to whisper, " Sigh ! "

Thomas William Parsons.

DANTE ALIGHIERI.

From the "Vita Nuova."

That which opposes in my mind doth die
  Whene'er, O beauteous Joy, I win thy sight:
  And I hear Love when I to you am nigh,
  Who saith, "Depart, if death doth thee affright."
My face the colour of my heart displays,
  Which, fainting, any chance support doth seek;
  And, as I tremble in my drunken daze,
  "Die! die!" the very stones appear to shriek.
Sin he commits who then may look on me,
  It my alarmëd soul he doth not aid,
  At least by showing that he feeleth grief
For that deep woe, which you deriding see,
  And which is in thy dying look displayed,
  Of eyes that long in death for their relief.

Charles Eliot Norton.

DANTE ALIGHIERI.

From the "Vita Nuova."

Love is but one thing with the gentle heart,
    As in the saying of the sage we find.
    Thus one from other cannot be apart,
    More than the reason from the reasoning mind.
When Nature amorous becomes, she makes
    Love then her Lord, the heart his dwelling-place,
    Within which, sleeping, his repose he takes,
    Sometimes for brief, sometimes for longer space.
Beauty doth then in modest dame appear
    Which pleaseth so the eyes, that in the heart
    A longing for the pleasing thing hath birth;
And now and then so long it lasteth there,
    It makes Love's spirit wide awake to start;
    The like in lady doth a man of worth.

Charles Eliot Norton.

DANTE ALIGHIERI.

From the "Vita Nuova."

To every heart that feels the gentle flame,
  To whom this present saying comes in sight,
  In that to me their thoughts they may indite,
  All health! in Love, our lord and master's name.
Now on its way the second quarter came
  Of those twelve hours, wherein the stars are bright,
  When Love was seen before me, in such might,
  As to remember shakes with awe my frame.
Suddenly came he, seeming glad, and keeping
  My heart in hand; and in his arms he had
  My Lady in a folded garment sleeping:
He waked her; and that heart all burning bade
  Her feed upon, in lowly guise and sad:
  Then from my view he turned; and parted, weeping.

Henry Francis Cary.

DANTE ALIGHIERI.

From the "Vita Nuova.

Ah, pilgrims! ye that, haply musing, go,
   On aught save that which on your road ye meet,
   From land so distant, tell me, I intreat,
   Come ye, as by your mien and looks ye show?
Why mourn ye not, as through these gates of woe
   Ye wend along our city's midmost street,
   Even like those who nothing seem to weet
   What chance hath fall'n, why she is grieving so?
If ye to listen but a while would stay,
   Well known this heart, which inly sigheth sore,
   That ye would then pass weeping on your way.
Oh, hear: her Beatrice is no more;
   And words there are a man of her might say,
   Would make a stranger's eye that loss deplore.

Henry Francis Cary.

DANTE ALIGHIERI.

From the "Vita Nuova."

Beyond the sphere that hath the widest gyre
   Passeth the sigh that leaves my heart below;
   A new intelligence doth love bestow
   On it with tears that ever draws it higher;
When it wins thither where is its desire,
   A Lady it beholds who honour so
   And light receives, that, through her splendid glow,
   The pilgrim spirit sees her as in fire;
It sees her such, that, telling me again
   I understand it not, it speaks so low
   Unto the mourning heart that bids it tell;
Its speech is of that noble One I know,
   For "Beatrice" I often hear full plain,
   So that, dear ladies, I conceive it well.

James Russell Lowell.

CINO DA PISTOIA.

WHY SIGHEST THOU?

"Why sighest thou?" Ah! ask not why;
   But late the tidings I have known,
   And all my wishes shattered lie:
   She, whom I love, from earth has flown,
And I am left behind, to sigh,
   To see her ne'er, to live alone:
   My sad life ending, death draws nigh;
   That, now to me, my heart has shown.
My eyes have lost their only light;
   On ladies they henceforth no more
   Can gaze, their one poor joy the sight
Of that dear house, that well-known door,
   Where they went oft, ere came the night
   To her, for whom my tears now pour.

Warburton Pike.

FOLGORE DA SAN GEMIGNANO.

On Knighthood (1).

This morn a young squire shall be made a knight;
   Whereof he fain would be right worthy found,
   And therefore pledgeth lands and castles round
   To furnish all that fits a man of might.
Meat, bread, and wine he gives to many a wight;
   Capons and pheasants on his board abound,
   Where serving men and pages march around;
   Choice chambers, torches, and wax candle light.
Barbed steeds, a multitude, are in his thought,
   Mailed men at arms and noble company,
   Spears, pennants, housing cloths, bells richly wrought;
Musicians following with great barony
   And jesters through the land his state have brought,
   With dames and damsels whereso rideth he.

                        John Addington Symonds.

FOLGORE DA SAN GEMIGNANO.

(II.)

Comes Blithesomeness with mirth and merriment,
   All decked in flowers she seemeth a rose-tree;
   Of linen, silk, cloth, fur, now beareth she
To the new knight a rich habiliment;
Head-gear and cap and garland flower-besprent,
   So brave they were May-bloom he seemed to be;
   With such a rout, so many and such glee,
That the floor shook. Then to her work she went;
And stood him on his feet in hose and shoon;
   And purse and gilded girdle neath the fur
   That drapes his goodly limbs, she buckles on;
Then bids the singers and sweet music stir,
   And showeth him to ladies for a boon
   And all who in that following went with her.

John Addington Symonds.

PETRARCH.

Love's Fidelity.

Set me whereas the sun doth parch the green,
  Or where his beams do not dissolve the ice :
  In temperate heat, where he is felt and seen ;
  In presence prest of people mad or wise ;
Set me in high, or yet in low degree ;
  In longest night, or in the shortest day ;
  In clearest sky, or where clouds thickest be ;
  In lusty youth, or when my hairs are grey :
Set me in heaven, in earth, or else in hell,
  In hill or dale, or in the foaming flood ;
  Thrall, or at large, alive whereso I dwell,
Sick or in health, in evil fame or good,
  Hers will I be ; and only with this thought
  Content myself although my chance be nought.

Earl of Surrey.

PETRARCH.

Love's Inconsistency.

I FIND no peace, and all my war is done;
    I fear and hope, I burn and freeze likewise;
    I fly above the wind, yet cannot rise;
    And nought I have, yet all the world I seize on;
That looseth, nor locketh, holdeth me in prison,
    And holds me not, yet can I 'scape no wise;
    Nor lets me live, nor die, at my devise,
    And yet of death it giveth none occasion.
Without eyes I see, and without tongue I plain;
    I wish to perish, yet I ask for health;
    I love another, and yet I hate myself;
I feed in sorrow, and laugh in all my pain;
    Lo, thus displeaseth me both death and life,
    And my delight is causer of my grief.

                    Sir Thomas Wyatt.

PETRARCH.

Soleasi nel mio cor.

She ruled in beauty o'er this heart of mine,
A noble lady in a humble home,
And now her time for heavenly bliss has come,
'Tis I am mortal proved, and she divine.
   The soul that all its blessings must resign,
And love whose light no more on earth finds room,
Might rend the rocks with pity for their doom,
Yet none their sorrows can in words enshrine ;
   They weep within my heart ; and ears are deaf
Save mine alone, and I am crushed with care,
And naught remains to me save mournful breath.
   Assuredly but dust and shade we are,
Assuredly desire is blind and brief,
Assuredly its hope but ends in death.

Thomas Wentworth Higginson.

PETRARCH.

QUAL DONNA ATTENDE A GLORIOSA FAMA.

Doth any maiden seek the glorious fame
Of chastity, of strength, of courtesy?
Gaze in the eyes of that sweet enemy
Whom all the world doth as my lady name!
   How honour grows, and pure devotion's flame,
How truth is joined with graceful dignity,
There thou may'st learn, and what the path may be
To that high heaven which doth her spirit claim;
   There learn soft speech, beyond all poet's skill,
And softer silence, and those holy ways
Unutterable, untold by human heart.
   But the infinite beauty that all eyes doth fill,
This none can copy! since its lovely rays
Are given by God's pure grace, and not by art.

Thomas Wentworth Higginson.

PETRARCH.

GLI OCCHI DI CH' IO PARLAI.

Those eyes, 'neath which my passionate rapture rose,
The arms, hands, feet, the beauty that erewhile
Could my own soul from its own self beguile,
And in a separate world of dreams enclose,
  The hair's bright tresses, full of golden glows,
And the soft lightning of the angelic smile
That changed this earth to some celestial isle,
Are now but dust, poor dust, that nothing knows.
  And yet I live! Myself I grieve and scorn,
Left dark without the light I loved in vain,
Adrift in tempest on a bark forlorn;
  Dead is the source of all my amorous strain,
Dry is the channel of my thoughts outworn,
And my sad harp can sound but notes of pain.

Thomas Wentworth Higginson.

PETRARCH.

LEVOMMI IL MIO PENSIERO.

DREAMS bore my fancy to that region where
She dwells whom here I seek, but cannot see.
'Mid those who in the loftiest heaven be
I looked on her, less haughty and more fair.
   She touched my hand, she said, "Within this sphere,
If hope deceive not, thou shalt dwell with me:
I filled thy life with war's wild agony;
Mine own day closed ere evening could appear.
   My bliss no human brain can understand;
I wait for thee alone, and that fair veil
Of beauty thou dost love shall wear again."
   Why was she silent then, why dropped my hand
Ere those delicious tones could quite avail
To bid my mortal soul in heaven remain?

Thomas Wentworth Higginson.

PETRARCH.

DICEMI SPESSO IL MIO FIDATO SPEGLIO.

Oft by my faithful mirror I am told,
And by my mind outworn and altered brow,
My earthly powers impaired and weakened now,—
"Deceive thyself no more, for thou art old!"
Who strives with Nature's laws is over-bold,
And Time to his commandments bids us bow.
Like fire that waves have quenched, I calmly vow
In life's long dream no more my sense to fold.
And while I think, our swift existence flies,
And none can live again earth's brief career,—
Then in my deepest heart the voice replies
Of one who now has left this mortal sphere,
But walked alone through earthly destinies,
And of all women is to fame most dear.

Thomas Wentworth Higginson.

PETRARCH.

DOLCI DUREZZE E PLACIDE REPULSE.

GENTLE severity, repulses mild,
Full of chaste love and pity sorrowing;
Graceful rebukes, that had the power to bring
Back to itself a heart by dreams beguiled;
   A soft-toned voice, whose accents undefiled
Held sweet restraints, all duty honouring;
The bloom of virtue; purity's clear spring
To cleanse away base thoughts and passions wild;
   Divinest eyes to make a lover's bliss,
Whether to bridle in the wayward mind
Lest its wild wanderings should the pathway miss,
   Or else its griefs to soothe, its wounds to bind;
This sweet completeness of thy life it is
That saved my soul; no other peace I find.

Thomas Wentworth Higginson.

PETRARCH.

The Buried Heart.

Not skies serene, with glittering stars inlaid,
Nor gallant ships o'er tranquil ocean dancing,
Nor gay careering knights in arms advancing,
Nor wild herds bounding through the forest glade,
   Nor tidings new of happiness delayed,
Nor poesie, Love's witchery enhancing,
Nor lady's song beside clear fountain glancing,
In beauty's pride, with chastity arrayed;
   Nor aught of lovely, aught of gay in show,
Shall touch my heart now cold within her tomb
Who was erewhile my life and light below!
   So heavy—tedious—sad—my days unblest,
That I, with strong desire, invoke Death's gloom,
Her to behold, whom ne'er to have seen were best!

Barbarina, Lady Dacre.

PETRARCH.

Love's Pilgrimage.

The palmer bent, with locks of silver grey,
Quits the sweet spot where he has passed his years,
Quits his poor family, whose anxious fears
Paint the loved father fainting on his way:
   And trembling, on his aged limbs slow borne,
In these last days that close his earthly course,
He, in his soul's strong purpose, finds new force.
Though weak with age, though by long travel worn:
   Thus reaching Rome, led on by pious love,
He seeks the image of that Saviour Lord
Whom soon he hopes to meet in bliss above:
   So, oft in other forms I seek to trace
Some charm, that to my heart may yet afford
A faint resemblance of thy matchless grace.

Barbarina, Lady Dacre.

PETRARCH.

Visions of Laura.

If, here reclining while I weep my woes,
    The turtle near me tells her plaintive tale,
Or headlong brook with warbling murmur flows,
    Or green leaves rustle to the sighing gale,—
In each low sound, that makes these rocks reply,
    I seem my Laura's long-lost voice to hear,
And oft, bright beaming on my raptured eye,
    Her charms more lovely than in life appear;
A Naiad oft, emerging from the flood,
    Graceful she seems to tread the dimpling wave,
Oft glides along, a Goddess of the wood,
    Oft sits, the Nymph of this sequestered cave,
Oft mounting beckons from a cloud of light,
Till Heaven at length receives her from my sight.

Thomas Russell.

PETRARCH.

A Stolen Glove.

Oh lovely hand, thou that my heart dost wring,
   And shut my life up in that narrow space,
   Hand, to which heaven and Nature, to win grace
Themselves, did all their zeal and cunning bring !
In yon five pearls of orient colouring
   (Though keen and cruel in my single case)
   Five taper fingers Love before my face
Hath bared awhile—what wealth on me to fling !
Oh white and dainty glove, oh glove, which hast
   Covered such roses fresh and ivory clear,
   Has mortal ever seen so sweet a prey?
I would I held her charming veil as fast ;
   But oh, the unfaithfulness of all things here !
   'Tis but a theft, and will be plucked away.

C. B. Cayley.

PETRARCH.

Two Roses.

Two roses, gathered with their dews in heaven
   ('Twas almost yesterday, the first of May),
Between two lovers, oh rare gift! were given,
   By one who long and wisely walked Love's way.
With pleasant words and with a smile that even
   Might teach a wild man gracious love—a ray
So soft and brilliant, that new colours driven
   Over the cheeks of both I saw straightway—
The sun amongst all lovers, thus he said,
   Smiling and sighing, *views not such a pair;*
     And then he clasped them both, and turned him thence.
Thus did they both his words and roses share;
This filled my harassed heart with joy and dread:
   Oh dainty day, oh happiest eloquence!

                   C. B. Cayley.

PETRARCH.

The Heart on the Hill.

Thou green and blooming, cool and shaded hill,
   Where sits, now songful, now in thought, thy guest,
   By whom the world's of glory dispossessed,
And heavenly spirits are made credible—
My heart, which quitted me for her (what skill
   He showed ; and if he come not back, shows best !)
   Goes on relating, how that foot hath pressed,
And how those eyes the sward are softening still.
He says, and with a shrug at every pace,
   " Oh were that caitiff here a little now,
   Who is so tired of tears and of his lot !"
She smiles, and how unequal is the case,
   I being heartless stone, and Eden thou,
   Oh hallowed, fortunate, delightsome spot !

C. B. Cayley.

PETRARCH.

Signs of Love.

If amorous faith, a heart of guileless ways,
  Soft languors, courteously controlled desire,
  And virtuous will, kindled with noble fire,
And lengthened wanderings in a lightless maze;
If thoughts, which evermore the brow displays,
  Or words that faint and brokenly suspire,
  Still checked with fear and shame; if hues no higher
Than the pale violet hath, or love displays;
If holding some one than one's self more dear,
  If sorrowing and sighing evermore,
  If chewing grief, and rage, and many a cross,
If burning far away, and freezing near,
  Are signs that Love consumes me to the core,
  Yours, lady, is the fault and mine the loss.

C. B. Cayley.

PETRARCH.

Quitting Vaucluse.

A LIFE of solitude I've ever sought
   (This many a field and forest knows, and rill),
   Lest among deaf and purblind wits, who ill
Have kept the road to heaven, I should be caught.
And if in this my will had gone for aught,
   Sorgue, amid many a fair, umbrageous hill,
   Might from the Tuscan airs detain me still—
Sorgue, that to help my tears and songs hath wrought.
But Fortune, being constantly my foe,
   Driveth me thither back, where much I fret,
   To see in mire my goodly treasure lie;
But to my hand, thence writing, she doth show
   More friendship; this may have some fitness yet;
   Love saw it, and my lady knows, and I.

C. B. Cayley.

PETRARCH.

On the Projected Crusade, 1333.

The successor of Charles, who with the same
   Great founder's diadem his locks hath dight,
   Already taketh arms, the horns to smite
Of Babylon, and him that bears its name;
And Christ's own Vicar will his home reclaim,
   And seek Bologna and Rome's imperial sight,
   Charged with his mantle and his keys aright,
If froward Fortune thwarteth not his aim.
Now will your meek and gracious Lamb the abhorred
   Wolves overthrow; and be this aye the fate
Of him that breaketh wedded Love's accord.
   Now comfort, therefore, her that hath to wait,
And Rome complaining 'gainst her absent lord,
   And your girt swords to Jesus dedicate.

C. B. Cayley.

BOCCACCIO.

On Dante Alighieri.

DANTE am I,—Minerva's son, who knew
   With skill and genius (though in style obscure),
   And elegance maternal to mature
My toil, a miracle to mortal view.
Through realms tartarean and celestial flew
   My lofty fancy, swift-winged and secure;
   And ever shall my noble work endure,
Fit to be read of men, and angels too.
Florence my earthly mother's glorious name;
   Stepdame to me, whom from her side she thrust,
Her duteous son,—bear slanderous tongues the blame!
   Ravenna housed my exile, holds my dust;
My spirit is with Him from whom it came,—
   A Parent envy cannot make unjust!

F. C. Gray.

LORENZO DE' MEDICI.

VIOLETS.

Not from the verdant garden's cultured bound,
   That breathes of Poestum's aromatic gale,
   We sprung; but nurslings of the lonely vale,
   'Mid woods obscure, and native glooms were found :—
'Mid woods and glooms, whose tangled brakes around
   Once Venus sorrowing traced, as all forlorn
   She sought Adonis, when a lurking thorn
   Deep on her foot impress'd an impious wound.
Then prone to earth we bowed our pallid flowers,
   And caught the drops divine; the purple dyes
   Tinging the lustre of our native hue :
Nor summer gales, nor art-conducted showers
   Have nursed our slender forms, but lovers' sighs
   Have been our gales, and lovers' tears our dew.

William Roscoe.

LORENZO DE' MEDICI.

CERCHI, CHI VUOL, LE POMPE.

SEEK he who will in grandeur to be blest,
    Place in proud halls and splendid courts, his joy;
    For pleasure, or for gold, his arts employ,
    Whilst all his hours unnumbered cares molest.
—A little field in native flowerets drest,
    A rivulet in soft murmurs gliding by,
    A bird whose love-sick note salutes the sky,
    With sweeter magic lull my cares to rest.
And shadowy woods, and rocks, and towering hills,
    And caves obscure, and nature's free-born train,
    And some lone nymph that timorous speeds along,
Each in my mind some gentle thought instils
    Of those bright eyes that absence shrouds in vain;
    —Ah, gentle thoughts! soon lost the city cares among.

William Roscoe.

LORENZO DE' MEDICI.

In Tears.

Ah, pearly drops, that pouring from those eyes
  Spoke the dissolving cloud of soft desire !
  What time cold sorrow chilled the genial fire,
  Struck the fair urns and bade the waters rise ;
Soft down those cheeks, whose native crimson vies
  With ivory whiteness, see the crystals throng ;
  As some clear river winds its stream along,
  Bathing the flowers of pale and purple dyes,—
While Love, rejoicing in the amorous shower,
  Stands like some bird, that after sultry heat
  Enjoys the drops, and shakes his glittering wings,—
Then grasps his bolt, and, conscious of his power,
  'Mid those bright orbs assumes his wonted seat,
  And thro' the lucid shower his living lightning flings.

William Roscoe.

LEONARDO DA VINCI.

Of Will, Power, and Duty.

Who would, but cannot—what he can, should will !
  'Tis vain to will the thing we ne'er can do;
  Therefore that man we deem the wisest, who
  Seeks not mere futile longing to fulfil.
Our pleasure, as our pain, dependeth still
  On knowledge of will's power; this doth imbue
  With strength who yield to duty what is due,
  Nor reason wrest from her high domicile.

Yet what thou canst not always shouldst thou will,
  Or gratified thy wish may cost a tear,
  And bitter prove what seemed most sweet to view:
Last in thy heart this truth we would instil,—
  Wouldst thou to self be true, to others dear,
  Will to be able, what thou oughtst, to do.

Samuel Waddington.

SANAZZARO.

Mors et Vita.

ALAS! when I behold this empty show
    Of life, and think how soon it shall have fled;
    When I consider how the honoured head
    Is daily struck by death's mysterious blow,—
My heart is wasted like the melting snow,
    And hope, that comforter, is nearly dead;
    Seeing these wings have been so long outspread,
    And yet so sluggish is my flight and low.
But if I therefore should complain and weep,—
    If chide with love, or fortune, or the fair,—
    No cause I have; myself must bear it all,
Who, like a man 'mid trifles lulled to sleep,
    With death beside me, feed on empty air,
    Nor think how soon this mouldering garb must fall.

James Glassford, of Dougalston.

MICHAEL ANGELO.

THE TRANSFIGURATION OF BEAUTY.

(A Dialogue with Love.)

NAY, prithee tell me, Love, when I behold
   My lady, do mine eyes her beauty see
   In truth, or dwells that loveliness in me
   Which multiplies her grace a thousandfold?
Thou needs must know; for thou with her of old
   Comest to stir my soul's tranquillity;
   Yet would I not seek one sigh less, or be
   By loss of that loved flame, more simply cold.—
The beauty thou discernest, all is hers;
   But grows in radiance as it soars on high,
   Through mortal eyes unto the soul above:
'Tis there transfigured; for the soul confers
   On what she holds, her own divinity:
   And this transfigured beauty wins thy love.

John Addington Symonds.

MICHAEL ANGELO.

Thanks for a Gift.

The sugar, candles, and the saddled mule,
   Together with your cask of malvoisie,
   So far exceed all my necessity
   That Michael and not I my debt must rule.
In such a glassy calm the breezes fool
   My sinking sails, so that amid the sea
   My bark hath missed her way, and seems to be
   A wisp of straw whirled on a weltering pool.
To yield thee gift for gift and grace for grace,
   For food and drink and carriage to and fro,
   For all my need in every time and place,
O my dear lord, matched with the much I owe,
   All that I am were no real recompense :
   Paying a debt is not munificence.

John Addington Symonds.

MICHAEL ANGELO.

The Garland and the Girdle.

What joy hath yon glad wreath of flowers that is
   Around her golden hair so deftly twined,
   Each blossom pressing forward from behind,
   As though to be the first her brows to kiss!
The livelong day her dress hath perfect bliss,
   That now reveals her breast, now seems to bind:
   And that fair woven net of gold refined
   Rests on her cheek and throat in happiness!
Yet still more blissful seems to me the band
   Gilt at the tips, so sweetly doth it ring
   And clasp the bosom that it serves to lace:
Yea, and the belt, to such as understand,
   Bound round her waist, saith: Here I'd ever cling.—
   What would my arms do in that girdle's place?

John Addington Symonds.

MICHAEL ANGELO.

THE DOOM OF BEAUTY.

Choice soul, in whom, as in a glass, we see,
   Mirrored in thy pure form and delicate,
   What beauties heaven and nature can create,
   The paragon of all their works to be!
Fair soul, in whom love, pity, piety,
   Have found a home, as from thy outward state
   We clearly read, and are so rare and great
   That they adorn none other like to thee!
Love takes me captive; beauty binds my soul;
   Pity and mercy with their gentle eyes
   Wake in my heart a hope that cannot cheat.
What law, what destiny, what fell control,
   What cruelty, or late or soon, denies
   That death should spare perfection so complete?

John Addington Symonds.

MICHAEL ANGELO.

Celestial Love.

No mortal thing enthralled these longing eyes
   When perfect peace in thy fair face I found;
   But far within, where all is holy ground,
   My soul felt Love, her comrade of the skies:
For she was born with God in Paradise;
   Nor all the shows of beauty shed around
   This fair false world her wings to earth have bound:
   Unto the Love of Loves aloft she flies.
Nay, things that suffer death, quench not the fire
   Of deathless spirits; nor eternity
   Serves sordid Time, that withers all things rare.
Not love but lawless impulse is desire:
   That slays the soul; our love makes still more fair
   Our friends on earth, fairer in death on high.

John Addington Symonds.

MICHAEL ANGELO.

Love, the Light-Giver.

With your fair eyes a charming light I see,
    For which my own blind eyes would peer in vain;
    Stayed by your feet the burden I sustain
    Which my lame feet find all too strong for me;
Wingless upon your pinions forth I fly;
    Heavenward your spirit stirreth me to strain;
    E'en as you will, I blush and blanch again,
    Freeze in the sun, burn 'neath a frosty sky.
Your will includes and is the lord of mine;
    Life to my thoughts within your heart is given;
    My words begin to breathe upon your breath:
Like to the moon am I, that cannot shine
    Alone; for lo! our eyes see nought in heaven
    Save what the living sun illumineth.

John Addington Symonds.

MICHAEL ANGELO.

Love's Entreaty.

Thou knowest, love, I know that thou dost know
   That I am here more near to thee to be,
   And knowest that I know thou knowest me :
   What means it then that we are sundered so?
If they are true, these hopes that from thee flow,
   If it is real, this sweet expectancy,
   Break down the wall that stands 'twixt me and thee;
   For pain in prison pent hath double woe.
Because in thee I love, O my loved lord,
   What thou best lovest, be not therefore stern :
   Souls burn for souls, spirits to spirits cry !
I seek the splendour in thy fair face stored ;
   Yet living man that beauty scarce can learn,
   And he who fain would find it, first must die.

John Addington Symonds.

MICHAEL ANGELO.

ON THE BRINK OF DEATH.

Now hath my life across a stormy sea
   Like a frail bark reached that wide port where all
   Are bidden, ere the final reckoning fall
   Of good and evil for eternity.
Now know I well how that fond phantasy
   Which made my soul the worshipper and thrall
   Of earthly art, is vain; how criminal
   Is that which all men seek unwillingly.
Those amorous thoughts which were so lightly dressed,
   What are they when the double death is nigh?
   The one I know for sure, the other dread.
Painting nor sculpture now can lull to rest
   My soul that turns to His great love on high,
   Whose arms to clasp us on the cross were spread.

*   John Addington Symonds.*

MICHAEL ANGELO.

A Prayer for Purification.

Perchance that I might learn what pity is,
   That I might laugh at erring men no more,
   Secure in my own strength as heretofore,
   My soul hath fallen from her state of bliss :
Nor know I under any flag but this
   How fighting I may 'scape those perils sore,
   Or how survive the rout and horrid roar
   Of adverse hosts, if I thy succour miss.
O flesh ! O blood ! O cross ! O pain extreme !
   By you may those foul sins be purified,
   Wherein my fathers were, and I was born !
Lo, Thou alone art good : let Thy supreme
   Pity my state of evil cleanse and hide—
   So near to death, so far from God, forlorn.

John Addington Symonds.

MICHAEL ANGELO.

Love's Justification.

Yes! hope may with my strong desire keep pace,
And I be undeluded, unbetrayed;
For if of our affections none find grace
In sight of Heaven, then wherefore hath God made
The world which we inhabit? Better plea
Love cannot have, than that in loving thee
Glory to that eternal peace is paid,
Who such divinity to thee imparts
As hallows and makes pure all gentle hearts.
His hope is treacherous only whose love dies
With beauty, which is varying every hour:
But, in chaste hearts uninfluenced by the power
Of outward change, there blooms a deathless flower,
That breathes on earth the air of paradise.

William Wordsworth.

MICHAEL ANGELO.

To the Supreme Being.

The prayers I make will then be sweet indeed,
If Thou the spirit give by which I pray:
My unassisted heart is barren clay,
Which of its native self can nothing feed:
Of good and pious works Thou art the seed,
Which quickens only where Thou say'st it may;
Unless Thou show to us Thine own true way,
No man can find it: Father! Thou must lead.
Do Thou, then, breathe those thoughts into my mind
By which such virtue may in me be bred
That in Thy holy footsteps I may tread;
The fetters of my tongue do Thou unbind,
That I may have the power to sing of Thee,
And sound Thy praises everlastingly.

William Wordsworth.

ARIOSTO.

IN WILL'S DESPITE.

How shall my cold and lifeless prayer ascend,
    Father of mercies, to thy seat on high,
    If, while my lips for thy deliverance cry,
    My heart against that liberty contend?
Do Thou, who knowest all, thy rescue send,
    Though every power of mine the help deny;
    And, oh, make haste before the hour draws nigh
    When to the gates of death I shall descend.
Eternal God, oh, pardon that I went
    Erring so long, whence have my eyes been smit
    With darkness, nor the good from evil known.
To spare offenders, being penitent,
    Is even ours;—to drag them from the pit,
    Themselves resisting, Lord, is thine alone.

James Glassford, of Dougalston.

PIETRO BEMBO.

"Ye Haunts Recluse."

Ye haunts recluse, where pleased I still retreat
   From crowds, and live alone, what spell denies
   My visit, now that Phœbus in our skies,
   Leaving the Twins, has gathered all his heat!
Nowhere so calm and free my heart will beat,
   Or thoughts so far above the earth can rise,
   Nowhere my spirit, fed with such supplies,
   Approaches nearer to its native seat.
How sweet it is in solitude to range
   I learned from thee; sweet when the world no more
   Distracts us, and our anxious fears are laid.
O wood and stream beloved, might I exchange
   This restless ocean and its burning shore
   For thy fresh waters and thy verdant shade!

                James Glassford, of Dougalston.

PIETRO BEMBO.

The Dream.

Sweet dream, to whom this stolen death I owe,
   That steeped my sense, and bade my sorrow fly,
   Say by what portal did'st thou leave the sky
A messenger of peace, to gladden woe?
What angel there had breathed of one so low
   That moved thee on the wings of love to fly?
   Since wearied and forsaken where I lie
None but thyself alone can help bestow.
Blest thou, who makest thus another blest,
   Save that you ply your wings in too much haste,
   And what you gave take back so soon again.
Ah, since the way you know, return at least,
   And sometimes of that pleasure let me taste,
   Which, but for thee, I would expect in vain.

James Glassford, of Dougalston.

VITTORIA COLONNA.

THE MASSACRE OF THE INNOCENTS.

PURE innocents, your lord, revealed so late,
   Departs, and leaves you unprotected quite;
   He wills that on your heads the storm should light,
   Averted from His own. Thrice happy fate!
Herod, his dark and fell revenge to sate,
   Crops the sweet flowers in bud! O baffled spite!
   He gives you thus unfading fruits and bright,
   And by short suffering, joys of endless date.
Snatched from the breast, not words but feeble cries
   Proclaim the martyrs, whom his deed hath crowned
   With palm and laurel from celestial groves.
No sooner are your silken shoulders found
   Fledged with the wing, O dear and infant loves,
   Than up to heaven at the first flight you rise.

                    James Glassford, of Dougalston.

VITTORIA COLONNA.

"Ye are the Branches."

Thanks to thy sovereign grace, O God, if I
   Am graffed in that true vine a living shoot,
   Whose arms embrace the world, and in whose root,
   Planted by faith, our life must hidden lie.
But thou beholdest how I fade and dry,
   Choked with a waste of leaf, and void of fruit,
   Unless thy spring perennial shall recruit
   My sapless branch, still wanting fresh supply.
O cleanse me, then, and make me to abide
   Wholly in thee, to drink thy heavenly dew
   And watered daily with my tears to grow.
Thou art the truth, thy promise is my guide;
   Prepare me when Thou comest, Lord, to show
   Fruits answering to the stock on which I grew.

James Glassford, of Dougalston.

FRANCESCO COPPETTA.

In Dreamland.

Of gold and diamond were the roof and wall,
   And windows sapphire, where my palace rose;
   With ivory gate, through which, as fancy chose,
   Went forth the dream that planned and built it all:
While from this perfect and so gorgeous hall
   Harmonious voices seem to float, like those
   Of quiring angels, and at every close
   Ravish the sense, and hold the mind in thrall.
At last I wake. But oh, how morning scowls
   On goodliest fabric which our sleep has reared!
   The lofty palace proves a dingy cot;
That heavenly music was from hooting owls;
   And where the gold and sparkling gems appeared,
   Lie heaps of straw, and worthless weeds that rot.

James Glassford, of Dougalston.

TOLOMEI.

THE EVENING STAR.

BLEST star of love, bright Hesperus, whose glow
   Serves for sweet escort through the still of night,
   Of Love the living flame, the friendly light,
   And torch of Venus when she walks below!
While to my mistress fair in stealth I go,
   Who dims the sun in orient chambers bright,—
   Now that the moon is low, nor cheers the sight,
   Haste, in her stead thy silver cresset show!
I wander not, these gloomy shades among,
   Upon the wayworn traveller to prey;
   Or graves dispeople with enchanter's song;—
My ravished heart from cruel spoiler's sway
   I would redeem: then, oh, avenge my wrong,
   Blest star of love, and beam upon my way!

Anon.

BERNARDO TASSO.

THE FOUNTAIN.

FREE to thy flocks, O wandering shepherd, still
   Are my green banks, with herb and flower inlaid,
   And free the olive and the mulberry shade,
   Whose aged boughs adorn this lovely hill.
But trouble not the crystal drops that spill
   From my clear fountain, by the muses made
   Sacred, nor these my sparkling springs invade,
   Whose cooling draughts the heavenly dream instil.
Here drinks Apollo, here the sister train,
   The loves unblemished, and the maidens chaste;
   Perchance a milk-white swan of gentle brood:—
If thou art ought but shepherd base and rude,
   Here may'st thou sing some sweetly moving strain,
   Then largely of my lucid waters taste.

James Glassford, of Dougalston.

GIOVANNI DELLA CASA.

To Sleep.

O Sleep, O tranquil son of noiseless Night,
   Of humid, shadowy Night; O dear repose
   For wearied men, forgetfulness of woes
   Grievous enough the bloom of life to blight !
Succour this heart that hath outworn delight,
   And knows no rest ; these tired limbs compose ;
   Fly to me, Sleep ; thy dusky vans disclose
   Over my languid eyes, then cease thy flight.
Where, where is Silence, that avoids the day ?
   Where the light dreams, that with a wavering tread
   And unsubstantial footing follow thee ?
Alas ! in vain I call thee ; and these grey,
   These frigid shades flatter in vain. O bed,
   How rough with thorns ! O nights, how harsh
      to me !

*   John Addington Symonds.*

ERASMI DI VALVASONE.

"Mormoranti Famosi."

Ye murmuring and fabled currents sweet,
   Fairer than crystal, more than crystal pure,
   So may the skies regard you, and secure
   From the fierce dog-star and his blaze of heat,
Still in these Alps your sparkling courses fleet
   No harm betide, nor any cloud obscure,
   Nor shepherd swain disturb, nor herd impure,
   Nor hostile thing your waters ever meet ;
Still may your faithful Naiads wear the crown
   Of happy love, and a perennial pride
   Wait on your banks, by Flora's finger wrought,—
If this my faithful look you carry down
   Upon the silver bosom of your tide
   To her who leads and tempers all my thought.

James Glassford, of Dougalston.

TORQUATO TASSO.

To Ferrante.

WITH thee, Ferrante, dauntless could I go
   To where the Tuscan waves the Spaniard greet,
   Whether the skies invite and winds are meet,
   Or loud and dark the angry tempest blow;
Could pass with thee where Atlas frowning low,
   Bathes in the bitter brine his rugged feet;
   Or where that youth, on stolen venture sweet,
   Sunk in the wave, a tale of tender woe;
Nor if to Afric sands, or Asian shore,
   You led the way, to follow would refuse,
   Baring my side to thousand armèd foes.
Yet weary as I am, and near my close,
   The wood, the fountain, and the secret muse,
   Are what I better love, and suit me more.

                James Glassford, of Dougalston.

TORQUATO TASSO.

Love.

Love, the great master of true eloquence,
  Disdains the tribute of a vulgar tongue:
  Cold are the words, and vain the affected song
Of him whose boasted passion is pretence.
  The favoured few that to his court belong
With noblest gifts the mighty god presents;
Their vigorous accents chain the admiring sense,
  And their warm words in torrents stream along.
  Oft too—O wondrous excellence of Love!—
Unuttered vows and sighs and accents broken
  With far more force the gentle bosom move
Than smoothest phrase with courtly action spoken.
  E'en Silence oft has found the power to prove
Both word and prayer, when it is true love's token.

J. Herman Merivale.

TORQUATO TASSO.

Love Unloved.

Ah! wherefore sigh for him who sighs not too?
    And love where love again will never grow?
    Why should these bitter tears incessant flow,
    While not one drop has wet the cheek for you?
Why pale for him that keeps his wonted hue?
    Why in your eye such beams of pleasure glow,
    While still you turn to one averted so,
    And gaze intent, with passion ever new?
If love, at will of others, lives or dies,
    Let this thy unrequited flame expire,
    And dim with grief no more these radiant eyes.
Let absence change thy tender heart to stone;
    Or, if it must be kindled, let the fire
    Light in thy breast, but not in thine alone.

James Glassford, of Dougalston.

TORQUATO TASSO.

TO A MATURE BEAUTY.

IN thy young spring, like some new-budding rose
    Wert thou, that from the wind's warm breathing hides
    In bashful maidenhood, and safe abides
    Within its leafy covert, soft and close ;
Or, since with thee may nothing vie that knows
    The touch of Death,—like some fair dawn that glides
    O'er dew-impearlèd fields, and down the sides
    Of golden hills in new-born beauty glows.
Now thy green spring is past, yet riper years
    Take naught from thee, nor can a lovelier one
    In youthful gladness smile at thy decay ;
More beautiful the perfect flower appears
    In odorous prime,—more glorious is the sun
    That crowns the broad arch of the bright noon-day.

Baroness von Gilsa.

TORQUATO TASSO.

SE D' ICARA LEGGESTI.

OFT have we heard, in Po's imperial tide
   How hapless Phaëton was headlong thrown,
Who durst aspire the sun's bright steeds to guide,
   And wreathe his brows with splendours not his own !
Oft have we heard, how 'midst the Icarian main
   Fell the rash youth who tried too bold a flight ;—
Thus shall it fare with him, who seeks in vain
   On mortal wings to reach the empyreal height.
But who, inspired by love, can dangers fear?
What cannot Love that guides the rolling sphere,—
   Whose powerful magic earth and heaven controls?
Love brought Diana from the starry sky,
Smit with the beauties of a mortal eye ;
   Love snatched the boy of Ida to the poles.

John Hoole.

MARINI.

Lux Umbra Dei.

Where shadowy wreaths of floating vapour 'bide,
    Buried in floods of unapproachëd light,
    In clouds of silence folded out of sight,
    Eternal wisdom doth her treasures hide;
And whoso with rash hand would draw aside
    Her veil, and read her laws, his vain and slight
    And human mind is crushed, and dazzled quite
    By lightning flash and thunder rolling wide.
O thou invisible Sun, who from our gaze,
    In that abyss of light no eye hath scann'd,
    That glory veilest with thine own bright rays,
Shine thou on me where poor and blind I stand,
    And let my dark night blossom to thy praise,—
    I know thee most when least I understand.

Baroness von Gilsa.

MARINI.

In Memoriam.

Here Leo rests. And ne'er was bred in Crete,
   Never in Sparta, or Molossian ground,
   Or wooded Thessaly, a nobler hound—
   Like thunder crashing, as the lightning fleet.
Not wolf or tiger did he fear to meet;
   And when from tuskèd boar he took his wound,
   The invader's muzzle, claws, and bones were found—
   A warrior's trophies scattered at his feet.
His drooping fellows, and the herd in heap,
   Who miss the Leader and Protector near,
   Wail him with piteous howl, and lowings deep.
Shepherds, who now the beast and robber fear,
   Unused without your guard the folds to keep,
   Strew flowers on Leo's turf, and drop a tear!

James Glassford, of Dougalston.

CHIABRERA.

THE ITALIAN PEOPLE.

WHEN Italy's proud heart imposed the yoke
  On the barbaric crew, and in the throng
  Of her pale slaves led captive kings along,
Triumphantly, to the old Tarpeian rock;
Not then her warriors girt them for the shock
  Of arms to cadence of Idalian song;
  But with a martial zeal; while deep and strong
O'er their fierce souls the tide of vengeance broke.
Lo! through the whirlwind, 'neath the lightning's glance,
Their thirsty spears, their iron limbs advance,
  Making earth terrible! We, day by day,
To dalliance, and sweet sound, and idle dance,
  Contented give our dastard souls away;
Prize of triumphant Force, each robber-despot's prey!

Sir Aubrey de Vere.

GIORDANO BRUNO.

The Philosophic Flight.

Now that these wings to speed my wish ascend,
   The more I feel vast air beneath my feet,
   The more toward boundless air on pinions fleet,
Spurning the earth, soaring to heaven, I tend :
Nor makes them stoop their flight the direful end
   Of Dædal's son ; but upward still they beat.
   What life the while with this death could compete,
If dead to earth at last I must descend?
My own heart's voice in the void air I hear.
   Where wilt thou bear me, O rash man ! Recall
   Thy daring will ! This boldness waits on fear !
Dread not, I answer, that tremendous fall :
   Strike through the clouds, and smile when death is near,
   If death so glorious be our doom at all !

John Addington Symonds.

TOMMASO CAMPANELLA.

THE WORLD'S A STAGE.

THE world's a theatre: age after age,
   Souls masked and muffled in their fleshly gear
   Before the supreme audience appear,
   As Nature, God's own Art, appoints the stage.
Each plays the part that is his heritage;
   From choir to choir they pass, from sphere to sphere,
   And deck themselves with joy or sorry cheer,
   As Fate the comic playwright fills the page.
None do or suffer, be they cursed or blest,
   Aught otherwise than the great Wisdom wrote
   To gladden each and all who gave Him mirth,
When we at last to sea or air or earth
   Yielding these masks that weal or woe denote,
   In God shall see who spoke and acted best.

John Addington Symonds.

TOMMASO CAMPANELLA.

The Human Comedy.

Nature, by God directed, formed in space
  The universal comedy we see ;
  Wherein each star, each man, each entity,
  Each living creature, hath its part and place ;
And when the play is over, it shall be
  That God will judge with justice and with grace.—
  Aping this art divine, the human race
  Plans for itself on earth a comedy :
It makes kings, priests, slaves, heroes for the eyes
  Of vulgar folk ; and gives them masks to play
  Their several parts—not wisely, as we see ;
For impious men too oft we canonise,
  And kill the saints ; while spurious lords array
  Their hosts against the real nobility.

John Addington Symonds.

TOMMASO CAMPANELLA.

The People.

The people is a beast of muddy brain
    That knows not its own force, and therefore stands
    Loaded with wood and stone ; the powerless hands
    Of a mere child guide it with bit and rein :
One kick would be enough to break the chain ;
    But the beast fears, and what the child demands,
    It does ; nor its own terror understands,
    Confused and stupefied by bugbears vain.
Most wonderful ! with its own hand it ties
    And gags itself—gives itself death and war
    For pence doled out by kings from its own store.
Its own are all things between earth and heaven ;
    But this it knows not ; and if one arise
    To tell this truth, it kills him unforgiven.

John Addington Symonds.

TOMMASO CAMPANELLA.

To Ridolfo Di Bina.

Wisdom and love, O Bina, gave thee wings,
   Before the blossom of thy years had faded,
   To fly with Adam for thy guide, God-aided,
   Through many lands in divers journeyings.
Pure virtue is thy guerdon : virtue brings
   Glory to thee, death to the foes degraded,
   Who through long years of darkness have invaded
   Thy Germany, mother of slaves not kings.
Yet, gazing on heaven's book, heroic child,
   My soul discerns graces divine in thee :—
   Leave toys and playthings to the crowd of fools !
Do thou with heart fervent and proudly mild
   Make war upon those fraud-engendering schools !
   I see thee victor, and in God I see.

John Addington Symonds.

TOMMASO CAMPANELLA.

The Book of Nature.

The world's the book where the eternal Sense
    Wrote his own thoughts; the living temple where,
    Painting his very self, with figures fair
    He filled the whole immense circumference.
Here then should each man read, and gazing find
    Both how to live and govern, and beware
    Of godlessness; and, seeing God all-where,
    Be bold to grasp the universal mind.
But we tied down to books and temples dead,—
    Copied with countless errors from the life,—
    These nobler than that school sublime we call.
O may our senseless souls at length be led
    To truth by pain, grief, anguish, trouble, strife!
    Turn we to read the one original!

John Addington Symonds.

TOMMASO CAMPANELLA.

THE MODERN CUPID.

THROUGH full three thousand years the world reveres
   Blind Love that bears the quiver and hath wings :
   Now too he 's deaf, and to the sufferings
   Of folk in anguish turns impiteous ears.
Of gold he's greedy, and dark raiment wears ;
   A child no more, that naked sports and sings,
   But a sly greybeard ; no gold shaft he flings,
   Now that fire-arms have cursed these latter years.
Charcoal and sulphur, thunder, lead, and smoke,
   That leave the flesh with plagues of hell diseased,
   And drive the craving spirit deaf and blind,
These are his weapons. But my bell hath broke
   Her silence. Yield, thou deaf, blind, tainted beast,
   To the wise fervour of a blameless mind !

*   John Addington Symonds.*

TOMMASO CAMPANELLA.

The True Kings.

Nero was king by accident in show;
   But Socrates by nature in good sooth;
   By right of both Augustus; luck and truth
   Less perfectly were blent in Scipio.
The spurious prince still seeks to extirpate
   The seed of natures born imperial—
   Like Herod, Caiaphas, Meletus, all
   Who by bad acts sustain their stolen state.
Slaves whose souls tell them that they are but slaves,
   Strike those whose native kinghood all can see:
   Martyrdom is the stamp of royalty.
Dead though they be, these govern from their graves:
   The tyrants fall, nor can their laws remain;
   While Paul and Peter rise o'er Rome to reign.

John Addington Symonds.

TOMMASO CAMPANELLA.

The Resurrection.

If Christ was only six hours crucified
   After few years of toil and misery,
   Which for mankind He suffered willingly,
   While heaven was won for ever when He died;
Why should He still be shown on every side,
   Painted and preached, in nought but agony,
   Whose pains were light matched with His victory,
   When the world's power to harm Him was defied?
Why rather speak and write not of the realm
   He rules in heaven, and soon will bring below
   Unto the praise and glory of His name?
Ah, foolish crowd! This world's thick vapours whelm
   Your eyes unworthy of that glorious show,
   Blind to His splendour, bent upon His shame.

John Addington Symonds.

SALVATOR ROSA.

Against those who would not believe him to be the real author of his Satires.

THEREFORE, because Salvator is my name,
    Do all and sundry "Crucify him!" shout?
    But well, it must be that the rascal rout
Should only after Passion yield me fame.
More than one Pilate asks me if I came
    At satire's crown by thieving out and out:
    Me Peters more than one deny and scout,
More than one Judas gives the kiss of shame.
A gang of canting and unhappy Jews
    Swear that with glory's sanctum making free,
I use another's Godhead in abuse.
But this time they shall find the thing askew:
They do the thieves, the Christ I shall not do;
    Rather my Pindus proves their Calvary.

William Michael Rossetti.

PETROCCHI.

I CALL on Time, who batters down that high
   And spacious pile, to say from whence it rose:—
   No answer he vouchsafes, but onward goes,
   And spreads his pinions broader to the sky.
Fame I invoke, *O thou, who lettest die*
   Things only of no worth, tell what are those!
   Troubled and sad her eye she downward throws,
   Like one oppressed who pours the deep-drawn sigh.
Then ruminating slow I turn aside;
   When on the ruined mass, with haughty brow,
   From stone to stone I see Oblivion stride:—
Perchance, I said, *thou knowest when or how!*
   But he in low and horrid thunder cried,
   I care not whose it was, mine it is now.

                  James Glassford, of Dougalston.

GIULIO BUSSI.

OF GLORY.

GLORY, what art thou? Thee, despite of pain,
  And want, and toil, the brave heart cherisheth:
  Thee the pale student courts, wasting, in vain,
  His primal youth, thy worshipper in death.
Glory, what art thou? Thine imperial breath
  Speaks woe to all: with pangs do men obtain
  An empty boon that duly perisheth,
  Whose very fear of loss outweighs the gain.
Glory, what art thou then? A fond deceit,
  Child of long suffering, empty air, a sweet
  Prize that is sought with toil, but never found:
In life, by every envious lip denied;
  In death, to ears that hear not a sweet sound:
  Glory—thou fatal scourge of human pride!

Sir Aubrey de Vere.

LODOVICO PATERNO.

Aure, O Aure! che'l ciel nudo e sereno.

Ye airs! sweet airs, that through the naked sky
   Fan your aurelian wings in wanton play;
   Or shedding quiet slumber, as ye fly,
     'Mid the dim forest murmuring urge your way;
To you these garlands, and this basket high
   Piled up with lily-bells and roses gay,
   And fragrant violets of purplest dye,
     Icon, all fainting in the noontide ray,
Scatters, a votive offering to your power:
   And oh! as ye receive the balmy spoil,
   Temper the inclement beam; and while his flail
He plies unceasing through the sultry hour,
   Hoarse Echo answering ever to his toil,
   Dispel the parted chaff with brisker gale.

Henry Francis Cary.

FRANCESCO REDI.

THE GARDEN OF EARTHLY LOVE.

OH! ye who follow Virtue, go not there!
   Those meadows are the flowery ways of Love,
   And he who there as Lord and King doth move
Is ever on the watch to trap and scare
The incautious hearts of all the young and fair,
   And if those sunny perilous ways ye prove,
   Your soul will flutter like a cagëd dove;
Oh! pause and taste not that perfumëd air!
Those shy white-breasted girls who smile and stand
With flower-bound hair, and singing, hand in hand,
   Along the roses, will lay wait for you,
   And clip your wings, and never let you through,
But shut your soul up in a thirsty land,
   And Love will come with them and mock you too.

Edmund Gosse.

FRANCESCO REDI.

THE CREATION OF MY LADY.

THAT Love,—whose power and sovranty we own,
  And who before all time was did beget
  The sun and moon and splendid stars, and set
All lovely things to speak of Him alone,—
Late looking earthward from his supreme throne
  Saw that,—although the beauty lingered yet,—
  The froward heart of man did quite forget
That all this beauty from His presence shone;
Wherefore, desiring to reclaim his eyes
  To heaven by some unequalled new delight,
He gave the world a treasure from the skies,
  My Lady's sacred beauty, pure and bright,
  Whose body is a robe of woven light,
And fashioned in the looms of Paradise.

Edmund Gosse.

FRANCESCO REDI.

GRIEF.

Sweet Ladies, who to Love your hearts incline,
    And hand in hand walk down compassion's way,
    Pause here an hour and weep with me and say
If ever there was sorrow like to mine !
My Lady had a heart that was the shrine
    Of every splendid truth that scorns decay,
    And round about her glorious limbs did play
Transcendent bloom, and from her eyes did shine
Such lights as flash about the aurioled head
    Of some divine fair angel in God's choir,
    And all her soul was like an altar-fire
With faith and love, and round her life was shed
    The silent chrism of innocent desire
And godlike grace ! Sweet Ladies, she is dead !

Edmund Gosse.

FRANCESCO REDI.

Love, the Musician.

Love is the Minstrel; for in God's own sight,
   The master of all melody, he stands,
   And holds a golden rebeck in his hands,
And leads the chorus of the saints in light;
But ever and anon those chambers bright
   Detain him not, for down to these low lands
   He flies, and spreads his musical commands,
And teaches men some fresh divine delight.
For with his bow he strikes a single chord
   Across a soul, and wakes in it desire
   To grow more pure and lovely, and aspire
To that ethereal country where, outpoured
From myriad stars that stand before the Lord,
   Love's harmonies are like a flame of fire.

Edmund Gosse.

FRANCESCO REDI.

The End of Earthly Love.

Love, thou hast had thy will with me ! oh ! say,
   What is there left for me to give thee more ?
Love, thou hast had thy will with me to-day,
   I can but give thee what thou hadst before !
Oh ! hungry Love, shall I devote my tears
   To quench this never-tiring old desire ?
Behold ! the sum of all my joys and fears
   Lies hidden behind thy quivering wings of fire !
What wilt thou more ?   Oh ! wilt thou that I die ?
   Behold my breast before thee strained and bare !
   Stab me to death, or wind my coils of hair
Around my throat and slay me where I lie ;
Crush me or kill me, tyrannous God and fair,
   But with thy kisses stifle my last cry !

Edmund Gosse.

FILICAJA.

Of Providence.

Just as a mother, with sweet, pious face,
    Yearns towards her little children from her seat,
    Gives one a kiss, another an embrace,
    Takes this upon her knees, that on her feet;
And while from actions, looks, complaints, pretences,
    She learns their feelings and their various will,
    To this a look, to that a word, dispenses,
    And, whether stern or smiling, loves them still;—
So Providence for us, high, infinite,
    Makes our necessities its watchful task,
    Hearkens to all our prayers, helps all our wants,
And even if it denies what seems our right,
    Either denies because 'twould have us ask,
    Or seems but to deny, or in denying grants.

Leigh Hunt.

FILICAJA.

Where, Italy, 's thine arm? or why seek'st thou
    From others aid? Alike thy foe, if right
    I deem, who guards thee, or who dares to fight;
    Both once thy slaves, both would destroy thee now.
Thus dost thou prize what yet the fates allow
    Of empire, thus that fame which shone so bright?
    Thus to thine ancient worth, which erst could plight
    His troth to thee, preservest thou thy vow?
Go, then; that ancient worth repudiate, take
    Sloth, and midst blood and groans and clamour dread,
    Sleep on, nor in thine utmost danger wake.
Sleep, vile adultress, till the murderous blade
    Vengeful shall on thine idle slumbers break,
    And pierce thee naked with thy minion laid.

                              Thomas Le Mesurier.

FILICAJA.

Buried Cities.

Here once ye stood, ye cities! now no more,
   In witness of your place, one stone remains,
   Where one may write, "Here oped the yawning
     plains,
   Here Syracuse, Catania stood of yore."
I o'er your doleful solitary shore
   You in yourselves oft seek, where only reigns
   A horrid stillness, that with sorrow drains
   My soul: my feet are check'd, my eyes run o'er.
And, oh! of wrath divine example dread!
   I cry,—I see thee, nor yet read thee right;
   Nor to thy awful dictates bow my head!
Then rise, o'erwhelmëd cities! bring to light
   The mighty wonder! let your huge bones spread,
   And strike each guilty age with just affright!

Thomas Le Mesurier.

FILICAJA.

"I AM STRICKEN, AND I AM THE BLOW."

No, not to thee nor to thy hate I owe,
   Nor ever did or ever shall, my shame;
   O fortune, I acquit thee of the blow,
   Not thy injustice or thy spite I blame.
I am both mark and shaft, and drew the bow;
   I forged the bolt, and lighted up the flame;
   And the black cloud whose peal has rattled so,
   From the dark smoke of my offences came:
Foul vapour from an impure heart that flows,
   And, issuing thence in exhalations thin,
   Recoils in thunder there from whence it rose.
Thus my reproach and grief turn all within,
   My guilt against myself the javelin throws,
   My sin the lash with which I lash my sin.

James Glassford, of Dougalston.

FILICAJA.

To Italy.

Italia, O Italia! hapless thou,
   Who didst the fatal gift of beauty gain,
   A dowry fraught with never-ending pain,—
   A seal of sorrow stamped upon thy brow:
O, were thy bravery more, or less thy charms!
   Then should thy foes, they whom thy loveliness
   Now lures afar to conquer and possess,
   Adore thy beauty less, or dread thine arms!
No longer then should hostile torrents pour
   Adown the Alps; and Gallic troops be laved
   In the red waters of the Po no more;
Nor longer then, by foreign courage saved,
   Barbarian succour should thy sons implore,—
   Vanquished or victors, still by Goths enslaved.

Anon.

G. CRESCIMBENI.

Io chiedo al Ciel.

I ASK the Sky, what new and daring foe
　With hand so high against his God rebelled?
　It answers, Man; and when he struck the blow,
　In blackness of eclipse the sun I held.
I ask the Ocean: heaving from below,
　Man, it replies; by Man He was compelled
　To suffer thus, and with convulsive throe
　Unwonted tides my lowest channel swelled.
I ask the Land: with long and bitter groan,
　Man shook me to the centre, is its cry;
　And still upon my face the marks are shown.
To Man, whose laughing hours in pleasure fly,
　To man, incensed I turn: proud Man alone,
　Tossing his lofty head, makes no reply.

James Glassford, of Dougalston.

GIOV. COTTA.

Love's Canticle.

"Cease," the belovëd said, "oh, cease from those
  Complaining sighs, fair one, and wipe the tear;
  Come to my side, thy lord invites thee near,
  Come reign with me, my dove, my pleasant spouse.

Winter is gone, again the damask rose,
  And lily sweet, and summer buds appear,
  And the loud north, which filled the flocks with fear,
  And sounded through the wood, no longer blows.

The turtle's tender voice is in the land,
  And calls the shepherd to his early care
  Among the vines, flitting from spray to spray.

Arise, celestial flowers for thee my hand
  Hath gathered, O thou fair among the fair;
  Arise, my love, my spouse, and come away."

James Glassford, of Dougalston.

GAETANA PASSERINI.

Genova Mia.

If still I can behold, and shed no tear
   Thy beauty, Genoa, mangled thus and torn,
   Think not thy son disloyal, whom the fear
   Of treason to thy state forbids to mourn.
Thy greatness in these ruins I revere,
   Trophies of stern resolve and generous scorn;
   At every step in every object near
   I trace thy courage in thy dangers borne.
Above all victory is to suffer well;
   And such is thine; with thee it still remains,
   Thus in the dust and not disconsolate!
Now Freedom loves upon thy form to dwell,
   And kisses every wound, and cries elate,
   O yes, the Ruins ever, not the Chains!

                    James Glassford, of Dougalston.

ZAPPI.

As toward the Ascrean mount I take my way
   Attending Glory at my right I hail ;—
   She cheers my heart, forbids my strength to fail,
And *On*, she cries, *for I with thee will stay.*
But as the long drear wastes our steps delay,
   Sudden doth Envy at my left assail,
   And says, *I too am here :*—her lips' dead pale
Speaks the black poisons on her heart that prey.
What then remains? If back my course I take,
   Envy, I know, that instant far is flown ;
   But then shall Glory too my side forsake.
With both will I the mountain's topmost height
   Resolve to gain : the one my toil shall crown,
   The other see it, and fret and burst with spite.

                            Thomas Le Mesurier.

ZAPPI.

THE STATUE OF MOSES.

WHAT form in everlasting marble wrought
   Sits, giantlike, Art's noblest triumph there?
   Voice almost trembles on the lip, high thought
   Seems throbbing on that brow of grandeur rare;
'Tis Moses!—Lo! that beard of wreathing hair
   And the twin glories from his temples shot;
   Moses!—but with that yet diviner air
   Upon the Mount from God's own presence caught.
Such was he once, when the wave's wild rebound
   Hung o'er him vast; such, when the deathful roar
   Of waters closed, at the command of Heaven!
And ye, vile crew,—once worshippers around
   A worthless calf; had ye but knelt before
   A shape like this, your sin almost had been forgiven.

                    Sir Aubrey De Vere.

METASTASIO.

Leggiadra Rosa.

O FAIR unsullied Rose, whose leaf was fed
   With sweetest dews, and drank the morning ray;
   Whose graceful bud now bending on the spray,
   Fanned by Aurora's breath, puts on the red;
That careful hand which plucks thee from thy bed
   Removes thee only to a brighter day,
   Where stripped of thorn, and never to decay,
   Thy choicer beauties may unmingled spread.
Thus art thou planted a perennial flower,
   Far from this fickle region full of gloom,
   Which winds disturb, and frost and sweeping shower.
A faithful Guardian tends thee now, by Whom
   Secured thou shalt combine, in peaceful bower,
   Immortal fragrance with immortal bloom.

James Glassford, of Dougalston.

FAUSTINA MARATTI.

The Rival.

Too beauteous Rival, whose enticing charms
   Once to my heart's sole Darling seemed so fair
   That oft he praises still thine ivory arms,
   Thy ruby lips, blue eyes, and auburn hair;—
Say, when he heard thy tongue's seducing strain,
   Stood he e'er silent, or with scorn replied,
   Or turned with altered brow of cold disdain
   From thy soft smiles, as now from mine, aside?
Once, once, too well I know, he held thee dear,
   And then, when captive to thy sovereign will—
   But why that look abashed, that starting tear,
Those conscious blushes which my fears fulfil?
   Speak, answer, speak; nay, answer not, forbear,
   If thou must answer that he loves thee still.

Thomas Russell.

CLEMENTI BONDI.

A Husband's Homily.

She whom you loved and chose, is now your bride,
   The gift of heaven, and to your trust consigned;
   Honour her still, though not with passion blind;
   And in her virtue, though you watch, confide.
Be to her youth a comfort, guardian, guide,
   In whose experience she may safety find;
   And whether sweet or bitter be assigned,
   The joy with her, as well as pain, divide.
Yield not too much if reason disapprove;
   Nor too much force; the partner of your life
   Should neither victim be, nor tyrant prove.
Thus shall that rein, which often mars the bliss
   Of wedlock, scarce be felt; and thus your wife
   Ne'er in the husband shall the lover miss.

James Glassford, of Dougalston.

CASTI.

The Debt of the "Giuli Tre."*

My Creditor seems often in a way
   Extremely pleasant with me, and polite;
   Just like a friend;—you'd fancy, at first sight,
   He thought no longer of the *giuli tre.*
All that he wants to know is, what they say
   Of Frederick now; whether his guess was right
   About the sailing of the French that night;
   Or, what's the news of Hanover and D'Estrèe.
But start from whence he may, he comes as truly,
   By little and little, to his ancient pass,
   And says, "Well—when am I to have the *giuli?*"
'Tis the cat's way. She takes her mouse, alas!
   And having purr'd, and eyed, and tapped him duly,
   Gives him at length the fatal *coup de grace.*

Leigh Hunt.

* Three sixpenny-pieces.

CASTI.

The Debt of the "Giuli Tre."

My Creditor has no such arms, as he
  Whom Homer trumpets, or whom Virgil sings,—
  Arms which dismiss'd so many souls in strings,
  From warlike Ilium and from Italy;
Nor has he those of later memory,
  With which Orlando did such loads of things;
  But with hard hints, and horrid botherings,
  And such rough ways,—with these he warreth me.
And suddenly he launcheth at me, lo!
  His terrible demand, the *giuli tre;*
  I draw me back, and thrust him with a *No!*
Then glows the fierce resentment of the fray,
  Till, turning round, I scamper from the foe;—
  The only way, I find, to gain the day.

Leigh Hunt.

PASTORINI.

To Genoa.

Proud city, that by the Ligurian sea
   Sittest as at a mirror, lofty and fair;
   And towering from thy curving banks in air,
Scornest the mountains that attend on thee;
Why, with such structures, to which Italy
   Has nothing else, though glorious, to compare,
   Hast thou not souls, with something like a share
Of look, heart, spirit, and ingenuity?

Better to bury at once ('twould cost thee less)
   Thy golden-sweating heaps, where cramp'd from light,
They and their pinch'd fasts ply their old distress.
   Thy rotting wealth, unspent, like a thick blight,
Clouds the close eyes of these;—dark hands oppress
   With superstition those;—and all is night.

Leigh Hunt.

VITTORELLI.

ON A NUN.

OF two fair virgins, modest, though admired,
   Heaven made us happy; and now, wretched sires,
   Heaven for a nobler doom their worth desires,
   And gazing upon *either*, *both* required.
Mine, while the torch of Hymen newly fired
   Becomes extinguish'd, soon—too soon—expires:
   But thine, within the closing grate retired,
   Eternal captive, to her God aspires.
But *thou*, at least, from out the jealous door,
   Which shuts between your never-meeting eyes,
   May'st hear her sweet and pious voice once more:
I to the marble, where *my* daughter lies,
   Rush,—the swoln flood of bitterness I pour,
   And knock, and knock, and knock—but none replies.

Lord Byron.

BETTINELLI.

VENICE.

WITH talons terrible, for slaughter spread,
   On wings that made a tempest of their way,
Down darting from the Alps, by vengeance led,
   The Hungarian falcon pounced upon his prey;
From wrath and rapine, trembling with dismay,
   The Italian doves before the Spoiler sped,
And wide o'er vale and mountain driven astray,
   Far from their ravaged homes for ever fled.

Then found the wiser halcyons' lovely brood,
   (Scared from their country, ruined and oppressed,)
A safe asylum on the rolling flood;
   By worth upheld, by liberty caressed;
'Mid thrones in ashes, cities sunk in blood,
   Ages on ages past,—behold the beauteous nest.

James Montgomery.

GABRIELE ROSSETTI.

STATUS QUO.

IN that same realm of rabid Belzebub,
    Who fits to every crime its punishment,
    Over a sink of unimagined scent
Lies Mauro Cappellari, visage *sub*.
And he, who was in life a moveless tub,
    Moveless immovable he there is pent:
    And aye for aye the Church's President
Sucks in an odour—*not* the one they dub
" Of sanctity."—" Another pain, and worse,"
    He one day said, " provide me : I can bear
No more the stink of all the universe."
But Belzebub to him replied, " No, no !
    Thou shalt remain to everlasting there !
This is the penalty of the *status quo*."

                         William Michael Rossetti.

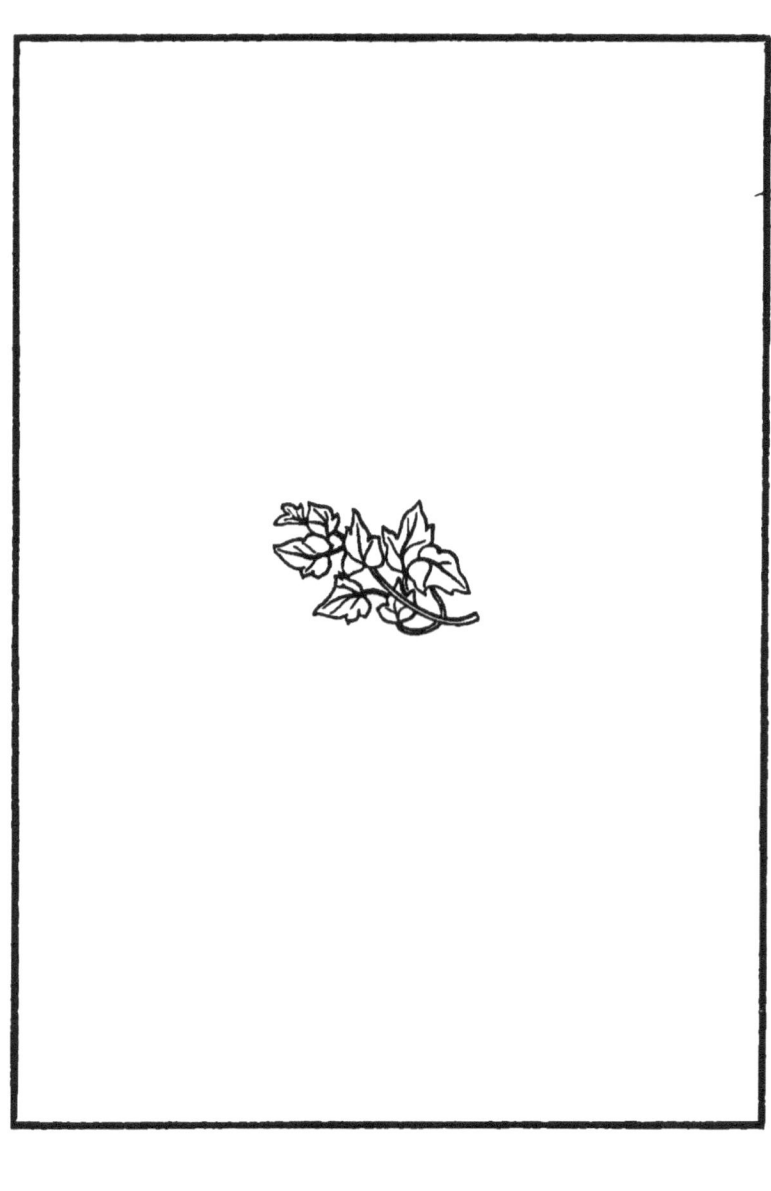

French Sonnets.

FRENCH SONNETS.

MELLIN DE SAINT-GELAIS.

The Sonnet of the Mountain.

When from afar these mountain tops I view,
I do but mete mine own distress thereby:
High is their head, and my desire is high;
Firm is their foot, my faith is certain too.

E'en as the winds about their summits blue,
From me too breaks betimes the wistful sigh;
And as from them the brooks and streamlets hie,
So from mine eyes the tears run down anew.

A thousand flocks upon them feed and stray;
As many loves within me see the day,
And all my heart for pasture ground divide.

No fruit have they, my lot as fruitless is;
And 'twixt us now nought diverse is but this—
In them the snows, in me the fires abide.

Austin Dobson.

RONSARD.

Voici Le Bois.

Here is the wood that freshened to her song;
   See here, the flowers that keep her footprints yet;
   Where, all alone, my saintly Angelette
Went wandering, with her maiden thoughts, along.

Here is the little rivulet where she stopp'd;
   And here the greenness of the grass shows where
   She lingered through it, searching here and there
Those daisies dear, which in her breast she dropp'd.

Here did she sing, and here she wept, and here
Her smile came back; and here I seem to hear
   Those faint half-words with which my thoughts are rife;

Here did she sit; here, childlike, did she dance,
To some vague impulse of her own romance—
   Ah, love, on all these thoughts, winds out my life!

Robert, Earl of Lytton.

RONSARD.

PAGE, SUY MOY.

FOLLOW, my Page, where the green grass embosoms
   The enamelled season's freshest-fallen dew;
   Then home, and my still house with handfuls strew
Of frail-lived April's newliest nurtured blossoms.

Take from the wall now, my song-tunëd lyre;
   Here will I sit and charm out the sweet pain
   Of a dark eye whose light hath burned my brain;
The unloving loveliness of my desire!

And here my ink, and here my papers, place:—
A hundred leaves of white whereon to trace
   A hundred words of desultory woe—

Words which shall last, like graven diamonds, sure;—
That, some day hence, a future race may know
   And ponder on the pain which I endure.

                Robert, Earl of Lytton.

RONSARD.

J'AIME LA FLEUR.

Two flowers I love, the March-flower* and the rose,
   The lovely rose that is to Venus dear,
   The March-flower that of her the name doth bear,
   Who will not leave my spirit in repose:
Three birds I love; one, moist with May-dew, goes
   To dry his feathers in the sunshine clear;
   One for his mate laments throughout the year,
   And for his child the other wails his woes:
And Bourgueil's pine I love, where Venus hung,
   For a proud trophy on the darksome bough,
   Ne'er since released, my youthful liberty:
And Phœbus' tree love I, the laurel tree,
   Of whose fair leaves, my mistress, when I sung,
   Bound with her locks a garland for my brow.

                              Henry Francis Cary.

---

* The violet, which the poet supposes to bear the name of his Marie.

RONSARD.

Avant qu' Amour.

Before that Love of drowsy Chaos rent
   The breast, and freed the light therein concealed,
   With land unshaped, and waters unrevealed,
   The very heaven was in confusion blent:
Even so my mind, of all things indolent,
   In the gross substance of my body sealed
   Lay all unformed, unwhole, till through my shield
   Love from thine eyes his piercing arrows sent.
My nature now by Love made perfect is,
   My heart is freed from all impurities,
   And Life to them and Power is given by Love.
Through my cold blood his subtle spirit stole,
   And rapt aloft by him, with him I move
   For ever joined in body, mind, and soul.

Cosmo Monkhouse.

RONSARD.

ROSES

I SEND you here a wreath of blossoms blown,
   And woven flowers at sunset gathered,
   Another dawn had seen them ruined, and shed
Loose leaves upon the grass at random strown.
By this, their sure example, be it known,
   That all your beauties, now in perfect flower,
   Shall fade as these, and wither in an hour,
Flowerlike, and brief of days, as the flower sown.

Ah, time is flying, lady—time is flying;
   Nay, 'tis not time that flies but we that go,
Who in short space shall be in churchyard lying,
   And of our loving parley none shall know,
Nor any man consider what we were;
Be therefore kind, my love, whiles thou art fair.

Andrew Lang.

RONSARD.

Of His Lady's Old Age.

When you are very old, at evening
   You'll sit and spin beside the fire, and say,
   Humming my songs, "Ah well, ah well-a-day!
When I was young, of me did Ronsard sing."
None of your maidens that doth hear the thing,
   Albeit with her weary task foredone,
   But wakens at my name, and calls you one
Blest, to be held in long remembering.

I shall be low beneath the earth, and laid
On sleep, a phantom in the myrtle shade,
   While you beside the fire, a grandame grey,
My love, your pride, remember and regret;
Ah, love me, love! we may be happy yet,
   And gather roses, while 'tis called to-day.

Andrew Lang.

RONSARD.

Another rendering of the same Sonnet.

When very old, at eve, while candles flare,
   Chatting and spinning by the fire you sit,
   And, marvelling, you hum the lines I writ,
Say: Ronsard sung me once when I was fair.

Then every serving-maid who slumbers there,
   Nodding above her task with drowsy wit,
   Hearing my name, will rouse at sound of it
And bless your name, your deathless praise declare.

A disembodied ghost, I shall have laid
My bones to rest beneath the myrtle shade,
   While you, a crone, crouch o'er the embers' glow,

Mourning my love, and your sublime disdain;
Live, trust me, wait not for to-morrow's pain,
   But cull to-day life's roses as they blow.

C. Kegan Paul.

RONSARD.

On His Lady's Waking.

My lady woke upon a morning fair,
   What time Apollo's chariot takes the skies,
   And, fain to fill with arrows from her eyes
His empty quiver, Love was standing there:
I saw two apples that her breast doth bear,
   None such the close of the Hesperides
   Yields; nor hath Venus any such as these,
Nor she that had of nursling Mars the care.

Even such a bosom, and so fair it was,
Pure as the perfect work of Phidias,
   That sad Andromeda's discomfiture
Left bare, when Perseus passed her on a day,
And pale as Death for fear of death she lay,
   With breast as marble cold, as marble pure.

Andrew Lang.

RONSARD.

HIS LADY'S DEATH.

TWAIN that were foes, while Mary lived, are fled:
   One laurel-crowned abides in heaven, and one
   Beneath the earth has fared, a fallen sun,
A light of love among the loveless dead.
The first is Chastity, that vanquishéd
   The archer Love, that held joint empery
   With the sweet beauty that made war on me,
When laughter of lips with laughing eyes was wed.

Their strife the Fates have closed, with stern control,
The earth holds her fair body, and her soul
   An angel with glad angels triumpheth;
Love has no more that he can do; desire
Is buried, and my heart a faded fire,
   And for Death's sake, I am in love with Death.

Andrew Lang.

RONSARD.

HIS LADY'S TOMB.

As in the gardens, all through May, the rose,
   Lovely, and young, and fair apparellèd,
   Makes sunrise jealous of her rosy red,
When dawn upon the dew of dawning glows;
Graces and Loves within her breast repose,
   The woods are faint with the sweet odour shed,
   Till rains and heavy suns have smitten dead
The languid flower, and the loose leaves unclose,—

So this, the perfect beauty of our days,
When earth and heaven were vocal of her praise,
   The fates have slain, and her sweet soul reposes;
And tears I bring, and sighs, and on her tomb
Pour milk, and scatter buds of many a bloom,
   That dead, as living, she may be with roses.

Andrew Lang.

RONSARD.

THE APPARITION.

I SHALL go wander dreaming, many a day,
   In this dear mead, wherein my love I met,
   While fear and hope my prison'd fancy fret,
Through her, whose eyes my will and wish obey:
What silken threads of shining tresses lay
   On her white neck I never can forget;
   The hues of rose and lilies haunt me yet,
With such soft changes on her cheek a-play.
She, I beheld, of any earthly dame
   Had not, good sooth, the forehead or the eyes:
It was no mortal down my meadow came;
An angel was this damsel, it is plain,
   My heart to snare, new-lighted from the skies:
No wonder was it I was captive ta'en.

Thomas Ashe.

RONSARD.

ON HIS ASTRÆA'S ARISING.

IN April month, whenas the new buds swell,
  The dawn not rises freshlier from the sea,
  Nor fairer shone the new-made deity
Of love, a-sail for Cyprus in her shell,
Than she I love above all words can tell,
  My sainted star, at morn arose for me:
  How laughed the heaven! and knowing it was she,
The flowers raised head to bless and greet her well!
The heaven-born Graces flitted round her brow,
And Youth and Love would low before her bow;
  But—this 'twas made my slavery complete—
No touch of art her beauty deigned to show:
The unfair face with art may fairer grow;
  Fair face without is ever fair and sweet.

Thomas Ashe.

JOACHIM DU BELLAY.

It was the time, when rest, soft sliding down
   From Heaven's height into men's heavy eyes,
   In the forgetfulness of sleep doth drown
   The careful thoughts of mortal miseries;
Then did a ghost before mine eyes appear
   On that great river's bank that runs by Rome,
   Which, calling me by name, bade me to rear
   My looks to heaven, whence all good gifts do come;—
And crying loud, *Lo! now behold*, quoth he,
   What under this great temple placèd is;
   Lo, all is naught but flying vanity!
So I, that know this world's inconstancies,
   Since only God surmounts all time's decay,
   In God alone my confidence do stay.

                              Edmund Spenser.

JOACHIM DU BELLAY.

On high hill's top I saw a stately frame,
    An hundred cubits high by just assize,
    With hundred pillars fronting fair the same,
    All wrought with diamond, after Doric wise;
Nor brick nor marble was the wall to view,
    But shining crystal, which from top to base
    Out of her womb a thousand rayons threw,
    One hundred steps of Afric golds enchase:
Gold was the parget; and the ceiling bright
    Did shine all scaly with great plates of gold;
    The floor of jasp and emerald was dight.
O, world's vainness! while thus I did behold,
    An earthquake shook the hill from lowest seat,
    And overthrew this frame with ruin great.

Edmund Spenser.

JOACHIM DU BELLAY.

Regrets.

Happy the man, like wise Ulysses tried,
Or him of yore that gat the Fleece of Gold,
Who comes at last, from travels manifold,
Among his kith and kindred to abide !

When shall I see from my small hamlet-side
Once more the blue and curling smoke unrolled ?
When the poor boundaries of my house behold,—
Poor, but to me as any province wide ?

Ah, more than these imperious piles of Rome
Smile the low portals of my boyhood's home !
More than their marble must its slate-roof be !

More than the Tiber's flood my Loire is still !
More than the Palatine my native hill,
And the soft air of Anjou than the sea !

Austin Dobson.

JOACHIM DU BELLAY.

Regrets.

ALAS! where now doth scorn of fortune hide?
And where the heart that still must conqueror be;
Where the strong hope of immortality,
And that fine flame to common souls denied?

Where is the joyance which at eventide,
Through the brown night the silver moon could see,
With all the Nine, whenas, in fancy free,
I led them dance, some sacred stream beside?

Dame Fortune now is mistress of my soul,
And this my heart that I would fain control,
Is grown the thrall of many a fear and sigh.

For after-time no more have I desire;
No more within I feel that ancient fire,
And the sweet Muses turn from me, and fly.

Austin Dobson.

JOACHIM DU BELLAY.

A Sonnet to Heavenly Beauty.

If this our little life is but a day
  In the Eternal,—if the years in vain
  Toil after hours that never come again,—
If everything that hath been must decay,
Why dreamest thou of joys that pass away,
  My soul, that my sad body doth restrain?
  Why of the moment's pleasure art thou fain?
Nay, thou hast wings,—nay, seek another stay.

There is the joy whereto each soul aspires,
And there the rest that all the world desires,
  And there is love, and peace, and gracious mirth;
And there in the most highest heavens shalt thou
Behold the Very Beauty, whereof now
  Thou worshippest the shadow upon earth.

Andrew Lang.

JOACHIM DU BELLAY.

To His Friend in Elysium.

So long you wandered on the dusky plain,
   Where flit the shadows with their endless cry,
   You reach the shore where all the world goes by,
You leave the strife, the slavery, the pain ;
But we, but we, the mortals that remain
   In vain stretch hands ; for Charon sullenly
   Drives us afar, we may not come anigh
Till that last mystic obolus we gain.

But you are happy in the quiet place,
And with the learned lovers of old days,
   And with your love, you wander ever-more
In the dim woods, and drink forgetfulness
Of us your friends, a weary crowd that press
   About the gate, or labour at the oar.

Andrew Lang.

JACQUES TAHUREAU.

Shadows of His Lady.

Within the sand of what far river lies
    The gold that gleams in tresses of my Love?
    What highest circle of the Heavens above
Is jewelled with such stars as are her eyes?
And where is the rich sea whose coral vies
    With her red lips, that cannot kiss enough?
    What dawn-lit garden knew the rose, whereof
The fled soul lives in her cheeks' rosy guise?

What Parian marble that is loveliest,
Can match the whiteness of her brow and breast?
    When drew she breath from the Sabæan glade?
Oh happy rock and river, sky and sea,
Gardens, and glades Sabæan, all that be
    The far-off splendid semblance of my maid!

Andrew Lang.

JACQUES TAHUREAU.

MOONLIGHT.

THE high Midnight was garlanding her head,
  With many a shining star in shining skies,
  And, of her grace, a slumber on mine eyes,
  And, after sorrow, quietness was shed.
Far in dim fields cicalas jargonéd
  A thin shrill clamour of complaints and cries;
  And all the woods were pallid, in strange wise,
With pallor of the sad moon overspread.

Then came my lady to that lonely place,
And, from her palfrey stooping, did embrace
  And hang upon my neck, and kissed me over;
Wherefore the day is far less dear than night,
And sweeter is the shadow than the light,
  Since night has made me such a happy lover.

Andrew Lang.

LOUISE LABÉ.

Long as I still can shed tears from mine eyes
   My bliss with thee regretting once again,
   And while my voice, though in a weaker strain,
Can speak a little, checking sobs and sighs,—
Long as my hand can tune the harmonies
   Of my bold lute to sing thy graces fain,
   And while my spirit shall content remain,
Thee understanding, nothing else to prize,

So long I do not yet desire to die;
But when I feel mine eyes are growing dry,
   Broken my voice, my hand devoid of skill,
My spirit in this its dwelling-place of clay
   Able no more to shew I love thee still,
I shall pray Death to blot my clearest day.

Arthur Hall.

ESTIENNE JODELLE.

The Ivy, Holly, and Green Bay.

I LOVE the bay-tree's never-withering green,
  Which nor the northern blast nor hoary rime
  Effaceth ; conqueror of death and time ;
  Emblem wherein eternity is seen.
I love the holly and those prickles keen
  On his gloss'd leaves that keep their verdant prime;
  And ivy too I love, whose tendrils climb
  On tree or bower, and weave their amorous screen.
All three I love, which alway green resemble
  The immortal thoughts that in my heart assemble
  Of thee, whom still I worship night and day.
But straiter far the knot that hath me bound,
  More keen my thorns, and greener is my wound,
  Than are the ivy, holly, or green bay.

Henry Francis Cary.

AMADIS JAMYN.

A Game at Football.

When I behold a football to and fro
   Urged by a throng of players equally,
   Who run pell-mell, and thrust and push and throw,
   Each party bent alike on victory;
Methinks I see, resembled in that show,
   This round earth poised in the vacant sky,
   Where all are fain to lay each other low,
   Striving by might and main for mastery.
The ball is filled with wind: and even so
   It is for wind most times that mortals war;
   Death the sole prize they all are struggling for:
And all the world is but an ebb and flow;
   And all we learn, whenas the game is o'er,
   That life is but a dream, and nothing more.

Henry Francis Cary.

PHILIPPE DESPORTES.

An Invitation.

This cool spring, and its waters silver-clean,
  In gentle murmurs seem to tell of love,
  And al! about the grass is soft and green ;
  And the close alders weave their shade above ;
The sidelong branches to each other lean,
  And as the west-wind fans them, scarcely move ;
  The sun is high in mid-day splendour sheen,
  And heat has parched the earth, and soiled the grove.
Stay, traveller, and rest thy limbs awhile,
  Faint with the thirst, and worn with heat and toil ;
  Where thy good fortune brings thee, traveller, stay.
Rest to thy wearied limbs will here be sweet,
  The wind and shade refresh thee from the heat,
  And the cool fountain chase thy thirst away.

Henry Francis Cary.

PHILIPPE DESPORTES.

L'Amour Fugitif.

This little child, young Love so blind,
His mother seeks him gone astray;
And as she seeks him she may find,
Hid in my heart, the runaway.

Betwixt the twain there's to my mind
No little danger in delay;—
The mother's dangerous I've divined,
And dangerous is the child they say.

He, if retained, will scorch my heart,
And if I bid him thence depart,
He still to me will cruel prove:—

Nay, in my heart, child, shalt thou stay;
Yet closer would I fold thee, Love,
So nestling burn less fierce, I pray.

Samuel Waddington.

THÉOPHILE DE VIAU.

SLEEP.

I'VE kissed thee, sweetheart, in a dream at least,
   And though the core of love is in me still,
   This joy, that in my sense did softly thrill,
The ardour of my longing hath appeased,
And by this tender strife my spirit, eased,
   Can laugh at that sweet theft against thy will,
   And, half consoled, I soothe myself, until
I find my heart from all its pain released.
My senses, hushed, begin to fall on sleep,
Slumber, for which two weary nights I weep,
   Takes thy dear place at last within mine eyes ;
And though so cold he is, as all men vow,
   For me he breaks his natural icy guise,
And shows himself more warm and fond than thou.

Edmund Gosse.

SCARRON.

THE BLACK DOUBLET.

YE monuments of human power and pride!
   Ye pyramids and tombs of structure vain!
   In you Art triumphs, human toils and pain
   Have vanquished Nature and her power defied—
Ye temples vast that ruins still abide,
   And thou, last pledge of Rome's imperial reign,
   Bold Coliseum! red with many a stain,
   Where Romans shouted while their victims died—
Time's hand shall drag you from your high estate,
   Nor of your boasted pride a vestige leave;—
   If marble then must yield its strength to fate,
Oh, let me not with thankless bosom grieve,
   If my black doublet, now of three years date,
   Shows my bare elbow through the ragged sleeve.

R. H. (Lon. Mag. 1820.)

MOLIÈRE.

TO MONSIEUR DE LA MOTHE LE VAYER,
UPON THE DEATH OF HIS SON.

LET thy tears flow, Le Vayer, let them flow:—
None of scant cause thy sorrowing can accuse,
Since, losing that which thou for aye dost lose,
E'en the most wise might find a ground for woe.

Vainly we strive with precepts to forego
The drops of pity that are Pity's dues;
And Nature's self, indignant, doth refuse
To count for fortitude that heartless show.

No grief, alas! can now bring back again
The son too dear, by Death untimely ta'en;
Yet, not the less, his loss is hard to bear,

Graced as he was by all the world reveres,
Large heart, keen wit, a lofty soul and rare,
—Surely these claim eternity of tears!

Austin Dobson.

FELIX ARVERS.

The Secret.

My life its secret and its mystery has,
    A love eternal in a moment born;
There is no hope to help my evil case,
    And she knows nought who makes me thus forlorn.

And I unmark'd shall ever by her pass
    Aye at her side, and yet for aye alone;
And I shall waste my bitter days, alas!
    And never dare to claim my love my own!

And she, whom God has made so sweet and dear,
Will go her way, distraught, and never hear
This murmur round her of my love and pain;

To austere duty true, will go her way,
And read these verses, full of her, and say,
"Who is this woman that he sings of then?"

Thomas Ashe.

FELIX ARVERS.

ANOTHER RENDERING OF THE SAME SONNET.

My soul its secret hath, my life too hath its mystery,
A love eternal in a moment's space conceived;
Hopeless the evil is, I have not told its history,
And she who was the cause nor knew it nor believed.
Alas! I shall have passed close by her unperceived,
For ever at her side and yet for ever lonely,
I shall unto the end have made life's journey, only
Daring to ask for nought, and having nought received.

For her, though God hath made her gentle and endearing,
She will go on her way distraught and without hearing
These murmurings of love that round her steps ascend,
Piously faithful still unto her austere duty,
Will say, when she shall read these lines full of her beauty,
"Who can this woman be?" and will not comprehend.

Henry Wadsworth Longfellow.

ALBERT GLATIGNY.

Before the Snow.

The winter is upon us, not the snow,
   The hills are etched on the horizon bare,
   The skies are iron grey, a bitter air,
The meagre cloudlets shudder to and fro.
One yellow leaf the listless wind doth blow,
   Like some strange butterfly, unclassed and rare.
   Your footsteps ring in frozen alleys, where
The black trees seem to shiver as you go.

Beyond lie church and steeple, with their old
   And rusty vanes that rattle as they veer,
A sharper gust would shake them from their hold,
   Yet up that path, in summer of the year,
And past that melancholy pile we strolled
   To pluck wild strawberries, with merry cheer.

Andrew Lang.

J. TRUFFIER.

THE BURIAL OF MOLIÈRE.

DEAD—he is dead! The rouge has left a trace
   On that thin cheek where shone, perchance, a tear,
   Even while the people laughed that held him dear
But yesterday. He died,—and not in grace,
And many a black-robed caitiff starts apace
   To slander him whose *Tartuffe* made them fear,
   And gold must win a passage for his bier,
And bribe the crowd that guards his resting-place.

Ah, Molière, for that last time of all,
   Man's hatred broke upon thee, and went by,
And did but make more fair thy funeral.
   Though in the dark they hid thee stealthily,
Thy coffin had the cope of night for pall,
   For torch, the stars along the windy sky!

Andrew Lang.

BAUDELAIRE.

The Day's End.

Under wan and hueless light,
   Life, that knows not rest nor shame,
   Runs or writhes without an aim;
So, when on the verge of sight
Rises the voluptuous Night,
   Making even hunger stay,
   Hiding even shame away,
Saith the poet, "O delight!
Rest at length for limbs and mind!
   With a weary heart that holds
   Nought but visions gloomiest,
Now I will lie down to rest,
   Wrapped within your curtained folds,
   Darkness comforting and kind!"

Arthur Reed Ropes.

BAUDELAIRE.

MEDITATION.

BE still, my sorrow, and be strong to bear;
   The evening thou didst pray for, now comes down,
   A veil of dusky air enfolds the town,
Bringing soft peace to some, to others care.
Now, while the wretched throngs of soulless clay,
   Beneath the pitiless sting of pleasure's whip
   Gather remorse in slavish fellowship,
Sorrow, give me thy hand, and come away,
Far from their noise. See the sad years deceased
   Lean from the sky in garb of bygone times,
   Regret that smiles up from the river's deep,
The sun that sinks beneath the bridge to sleep,
   And hear the footsteps of the Night that climbs
   Like a long shroud, trailing across the East.

Arthur Reed Ropes.

BAUDELAIRE.

THE REBEL.

An angel swoops like eagle on his prey,
   Grips by the hair the unbelieving wight,
   And furious cries, "O scorner of the right,
'Tis I, thine Angel good, who speaks. Obey!
Know, thou shalt love without the least distaste
   The poor, the base, the crooked and the dull;
   So shall the pageant of thy Lord be graced
With banners by thy love made beautiful.
This is God's love. See that thy soul be fired
   With its pure flame or e'er thy heart grow tired,
   And thou shalt know the bliss that lasts for aye."
Ah! with what ruthless love that Angel grand
   Tortures and racks the wretch with giant hand!
   —But still he answers "Never, till I die."

Cosmo Monkhouse.

SULLY PRUDHOMME.

The Shadow.

We walk: our shadow follows in the rear,
Mimics our motions, treads where'er we tread,
Looks without seeing, listens without an ear,
Crawls while we walk with proud uplifted head.

Like to his shadow, man himself down here,
A little living darkness, a frail shred
Of form, sees, speaks, but with no knowledge clear,
Saying to Fate, "By thee my feet are led."

Man shadows but a lower angel who,
Fallen from high, is but a shadow too;
So man himself an image is of God.

And, maybe, in some place by us untrod,
Near deepest depths of nothingness or ill,
Some wraith of human wraiths grows darker still.

Arthur O'Shaughnessy.

SULLY PRUDHOMME

PROFANATION.

BEAUTY, that mak'st the body like a fane,
What gods have spurned thee, since thou fall'st thus low,
Lending thyself to harlots and thy glow
To deck dead hearts that cannot live again?

Made for the chaste and strong, didst thou in vain
Seek strength and purity, round such to throw
Thy glorious garb aright? and is it so
Thou robest sin and hidest falsehood's stain?

Fly back to heaven; profane no more thy worth,
Nor drag down love and genius to base kneeling
At feet of courtezans when thee they seek.

Quit the white flock of women; and henceforth
Form shall be moulded upon truth, revealing
The soul, and truth upon the brow shall speak.

Arthur O'Shaughnessy.

SULLY PRUDHOMME.

The Struggle.

Nightly tormented by returning doubt,
I dare the Sphinx with faith and unbelief;
And through lone hours when no sleep brings relief
The monster rises all my hopes to flout.

In a still agony, the light blown out,
I wrestle with the Unknown: nor long nor brief
The night appears, my narrow couch of grief
Grown like the grave with Death walled round about.

Sometimes my mother, coming with her lamp,
Seeing my brow as with a death-sweat damp,
Asks, "Ah, what ails thee, child? hast thou no rest?"

And then I answer, touched by her look of yearning,
Holding my beating heart and forehead burning,
"Mother, I strove with God, and was hard prest."

Arthur O'Shaughnessy.

SULLY PRUDHOMME.

The Appointment.

'Tis late; the astronomer in his lonely height,
Exploring all the dark, descries afar
Orbs that like distant isles of splendour are,
And mornings whitening in the infinite.

Like winnowed grain the worlds go by in flight,
Or swarm in glistening spaces nebular;
He summons one dishevelled wandering star,—
Return ten centuries hence on such a night.

The star will come. It dare not by one hour
Cheat Science, or falsify her calculation;
Men will have passed, but watchful in the tower

Man shall remain in sleepless contemplation;
And should all men have perished there in turn,
Truth in their place would watch that star's return.

Arthur O'Shaughnessy.

German Sonnets.

GERMAN SONNETS.

BÜRGER.

THE HEART WITHOUT A HOME.

LONG like a dove by the fierce falcon driven,
   Hither and thither wandered sad my Love;—
   And simply it imagined, like a dove,
That it had reached at length its tranquil heaven.
Ah, Faith! to fond delusions vainly given;
   And Fate! conceived by none but those who prove;
   That home from which it dreaded no remove
Is by the instant stroke of lightning riven!

Hither and thither still it wanders now;
   Poor little dove! 'twixt earth and heaven remains
No object for its wing;—the Fates allow
   No kindred Heart in solace of its pains;
   Not one this desolated Earth contains
That might return its warmth, that might reward its vow.
                                   Capel Lofft.

GOETHE.

THE MAIDEN SPEAKS.

How grave thou lookest, loved one,—wherefore so?
   Thy marble image seems a type of thee ;—
   Like it, no sign of life thou giv'st to me ;
Compared with thee, the stone appears to glow.

Behind his shield in ambush lurks the foe,
   The *friend's* brow all-unruffled should we see :
   I seek thee, but thou seek'st away to flee ;—
Fixed as this sculptured figure, learn to grow !

Tell me, to which should I the preference pay?
   Must I from both with coldness meet alone?
   This one is lifeless, thou with life art blest.

In short, no longer to throw words away,
   I'll fondly kiss, and kiss, and kiss this stone,
   Till thou dost tear me hence with envious breast.

Edgar Alfred Bowring.

GOETHE.

To a Golden Heart, Worn Round His Neck.

Remembrancer of joys long passed away,
    Relic, from which as yet I cannot part,
O, hast thou power to lengthen love's short day?
    Stronger thy chain than that which bound the heart?

Lili, I fly!—yet still thy fetters press me
    In distant valley, or far lonely wood.
Still with a struggling sigh of pain confess thee
    The mistress of my soul in every mood.

The bird may burst the silken chain that bound him,
    Flying to the green home, which fits him best;
But, ah! he bears the prisoner's badge around him,
    Still by the piece about his neck distressed.
He ne'er can breathe his free wild notes again;
They're stifled by the pressure of his chain.

Margaret Fuller Ossoli.

CHRISTOPH AUGUST TIEDGE.

In Memoriam (THEODOR KÖRNER).

I.

PROUDLY, e'en now, the young oak waved on high,
   Hung round with youthful green full gorgeously;
   And calmly graceful, and yet bold and free,
Reared its majestic head in upper sky.
   Hope said, "How great, in coming days, shall be
That tree's renown!" Already, far or nigh,
No monarch of the forest towered so high:
   The trembling leaves murmured melodiously
As love's soft whisper; and its branches rung
   As if the master of the tuneful string,
Mighty Apollo, there his lyre had hung.
But, ah, it sank. A storm had bowed its pride!—
   Alas! untimely snatched in life's green spring,
My noble youth, the bard and hero, died!

Charles T. Brooks.

II.

Where sleeps my youth upon his country's breast?
   Show me the place where ye have laid him down;
'Mid his own music's echoes let him rest,
   And in the brightness of his fair renown.
Large was his heart; his free soul heavenward pressed;
   Alternate songs and deeds his brow did crown.
Where sleeps my youth upon his country's breast?
   Show me the place where ye have laid him down.
"The youth lies slumbering where the battle-ground
   Drank in the blood of noble hearts like rain;"
There, youthful hero, in thine ear shall sound
   A grateful echo of thy harp's last strain:
"O Father bless thou me!"* shall ring again;
That blessing thou in calmer world hast found.

Charles T. Brooks.

---

* Quoted from Körner's "Prayer during Battle."

III.

Ye who so keenly mourn the loved one's death,
  Go with me to the mound that marks his grave,
And breathe awhile the consecrated breath
  Of the old oak whose boughs high o'er him wave.
  Sad Friendship there hath laid the young and brave;
Her hand shall guide us thither. Hark! she saith,
  "Beneath the hallowed oak's cool, peaceful breath
  These hands had dug the hero's silent grave:
Yet were the dear remains forbid to rest
Where lip to lip in bloody strife was pressed,
  And ghastly death stares from the mouldering heap;
A statelier tomb that sacred dust must keep;
A German prince hath spoken: This new guest,
  And noblest, in a princely hall shall sleep."

Charles T. Brooks.

IV.

THERE rests the Muses' son—his conflicts o'er :
   Forget him not, my German country, thou !
   The wreath that twined around his youthful brow
May deck his urn,—but him, alas ! no more.
Dost ask, thou herdsmaid, for those songs of yore?
   Though fled his form, his soul is with us now,
And ye who mourn the hero gone before,
   Here on his grave renew the patriot vow ;
Through Freedom's holy struggle he hath made,
   Ye noble German sons, his heavenward way.
   Feel what he felt, while bending o'er his clay ;
Thus honour him, while, in the green-arched shade,
Sweet choirs of nightingales, through grove and glade,
   Awake the memory of his kindling lay.

Charles T. Brooks.

KÖRNER.

Rauch's Bust of Queen Louisa.

How soft thy sleep !—The tranquil features seem
   To breathe again thy life's fair dreams e'en now;
   'Tis Slumber droops his wings around thy brow,
And sacred Peace hath veiled the eye's pure beam.
   So slumber on, till, O my country ! thou,
While beacon-smoke from every hill doth stream,
And the long-rusted swords, impatient, gleam,
   Shalt raise to heaven the patriot's holy vow.
Down, down through night and death, God's way may lie;
   Yet this must be our hope—our battle-cry:
   Our children's children shall as freemen die !
When Freedom's morning, bloody-red, shall break,
Then, for thy bleeding, praying country's sake,
Then, German wife, our guardian angel, wake !

                              Charles T. Brooks.

CHAMISSO.

LAST SONNET.

THEY say the year is in its summer glory:
   But thou, O Sun, appearest chill and pale,
   The vigour of thy youth begins to fail,—
Say, art thou, too, becoming old and hoary?
Old Age, forsooth!—what profits our complaining?
   Although a bitter guest and comfortless,
   One learns to smile beneath its stern caress,
The fated burden manfully sustaining:
'Tis only for a span, a summer's day.
   Deep in the fitful twilight have I striven,
   Must now the even-feast of rest be holding:
One curtain falls,—and, lo! another play!
   "His will be done whose mercy much has given?"
   I'll pray,—my grateful hands to heaven folding.

Anon.

J. W. LUDWIG GLEIM.

Cynthia Bathing.

From her fair limbs the last thin veil she drew,
    And naked stood in all her charms confess'd,
The wanton gales her ringlets backward blew,
    To sport themselves more freely on her breast:
From each warm beauty of the uncovered maid,
    Before scarce guessed at, or but seen in part,
From all, for all was to my eyes displayed,
    Delicious poison trickled to my heart:
Since thus I gazed, (was mine to gaze the blame?),
    Nor bliss my soul hath tasted, nor repose;
The subtle venom glides through all my frame,
    And in my brain a fiery deluge glows:
Thou, who my pangs wouldst shun, with wiser care
The spot, where Cynthia bathes at noon, beware.

Thomas Russell.

A. G. VON PLATEN-HALLERMÜNDE.

FAIR as the day that bodes as fair a morrow,
  With noble brow, with eyes in heaven's dew,
  Of tender years, and charming as the new,
So found I thee,—so found I, too, my sorrow.
O, could I shelter in thy bosom borrow,
  There most collected where the most unbent!
  O, would this coyness were already spent,
That aye adjourns our union till to-morrow!
But canst thou hate me? Art thou yet unshaken?
  Wherefore refusest thou the soft confession
To him who loves, yet feels himself forsaken?
  Oh, when thy future love doth make expression,
An anxious rapture will the moment waken,
  As with a youthful prince at his accession.

Anon.

UHLAND.

THE DEATH-ANGEL.

How is it with the dying, who can say?
   Yet wondrously it seized me yesternight,
   My limbs already sank in death's cold might,
Within my breast the last pulse ebbed away:
Upon my spirit fell a strange dismay;
   The mind, that ever felt securely bright,
   Now flickering low, now fanned again to light,
Its feeble flame to every wind a prey!
Say, was it but an evil dream to prove me?
   The lark sings loud, the rosy morn is glowing,
And new desire to stirring life doth move me;—
Or passed indeed the pale Death-angel here?
   These flowers that yesternight were freshly blowing
Now from their stalks hang withered, dead, and sere.

Matilda Dickson.

UHLAND.

The Two Maidens.

I saw two maidens on the mountain height,
   Their faces lovely as their forms were fair;
   They seemed to scan the western fields of air,
   And sat in fond and sisterly delight.
I saw the lovely right arm raised by one
   While pointing over mount, and stream, and lea;
   The other held, that she might better see,
   Her left arm interposed before the sun.

No wonder then that hope put forth its snare,
   And that the sweet wish ventured to intrude—
   O would that either place 'twere mine to win!
Yet when I view'd again that tender pair,
   I fain confessed, with feelings more subdued,
   Ah, surely no,—to part them were a sin.

                              Alexander Platt.

UHLAND.

THE CRITIC'S CONVERSION TO THE SONNET.

THOU, who but lately from the Critic's stool,
   So sorely jaded us poor sonneteers,
   And, spurting fire and gall about our ears,
   Did'st execrate us to Hell's lowest pool;—
Thou spotless ermine of the olden school,
   O, what a blot thy snow-white hide besmears!
   Thou 'st toodled forth a sonnet, it appears,
   A whining sigh to win a lady-fool!

Hast thou forgot thy proffer'd admonition?
   Forgot what veteran Voss, so oft dictating,
   Half-angrily, half-jestingly, enjoined?
Forsooth, thou 'rt very like a new edition
   Of him, who gave his pilfering boy a rating,
   And then chopped up the cherries he'd purloined.

                            Alexander Platt.

LEIPZIG, 1848.

HEINRICH HEINE.

Fresco-Sonnets to Christian S——.

A HAUNTING tale that will not be denied
   Besets me,—in that tale a tender lay,
   Amid whose music, blooming like the may
A wondrous lovely little maid doth glide;
Within the maid a small heart doth abide,
   But in that heart no sparks of love can glow;
   Within that loveless nature cold as snow,
Dwell only arrogance and frozen pride.
—Hear'st thou how rings that story thro' my brain,
   And how that song its sad refrain is blending,
   And how the maiden titters, soft and low?
I only fear my heart will burst in twain;
   And oh! that were, methinks, a fearful ending
     Should I go mad with all this weight of woe.

Matilda Dickson.

HEINRICH HEINE.

FRESCO-SONNETS TO CHRISTIAN S——.

BEWARE, my friend, of fiends' grimaces dire,
Yet worse are gentle smiling angel faces.
One such did tempt me once with sweet embraces,
But felt I her sharp claws as I drew nigh her.
And old black cats, my friend, beware their ire,
Yet worse are white young kittens in some cases.
One such I treasured whilom for her graces,
Yet was my heart much lacerated by her.
O pretty minx! O rare sweet little maiden!
How could that limpid eye of thine deceive me?
How could that little paw a heart-wound leave me?
O rare soft kitten-paw with velvet laden!
Would I might press thee to my lips all glowing,
Tho' from my heart were e'en its life-blood flowing!

Stratheir.

HEINRICH HEINE.

To My Mother.

(1.)

I've kept a haughty heart thro' grief and mirth,
And borne my head perchance a thought too high;
If even a king should look me in the eye
I would not bend it humbly to the earth :
Yet, dearest mother, such the gentle worth
Of thy benignant presence, angel-mild,
It ever hath my proudest moods beguiled,
And given to softer, humbler feelings birth.
Was it thy mind's calm penetrative power,
Thy purer mind, that secretly came o'er me,
And unto Heaven's clearer light upbore me;
Or did remembrance sting me in that hour,
With thought of words and deeds which pierced unkindly
That gentle heart, loving me still so blindly.

Matilda Dickson.

HEINRICH HEINE.

TO MY MOTHER

(II.)

IN a wild mood of yore I left thee, turning
Throughout the ends of the wide earth to wander,
To seek a love that I might meet with fonder,
And clasp it with love's own ecstatic burning.
Through every path I followed love with yearning,
With out-stretched hands before each door-step yonder,
I begged a dole of love that men do squander,—
Yet met with but cold hate and laughter spurning.
Still ever roamed I in love's quest, and ever
I followed love, and yet did find love never,
And home returned again, heart-sick and rueing.
But thou didst come in welcome forth to meet me,
And, oh! within thy swimming eyes did greet me
The sweet love I had been so long pursuing.

Stratheir.

HEINRICH HEINE.

Fresco-Sonnets to Christian S——.

FAIN would I weep, but, ah, I cannot weep;
   Fain would I upward full of vigour spring,
   But cannot; to the earth I needs must cling,
Spurned by the reptiles that around me creep.
Fain would I near my beauteous mistress keep,
   Near my bright light of life be hovering,
   And in her clear sweet breath be revelling,
But cannot; for my heart with sorrow deep
Is breaking; from my broken heart doth flow
   My burning blood, my strength within me fades,
   And darker, darker grows the world to me.
   With secret awe I yearn unceasingly
For yonder misty realm, where silent shades
Their gentle loving arms around me throw.

Edgar Alfred Bowring.

Spanish Sonnets.

M*

SPANISH SONNETS.

FROM THE ROMANCERO

DE MIGUEL DE MADRIGAL.

HAD I a thousand souls with which to love thee,
   I'd throw them all, delighted, at thy feet ;
Had I uncounted gold wherewith to move thee,
   'Twould seem unworthy all, and incomplete :
I fain would be an Argus but to view thee,
   And a Briareus round thy charms to cling ;
Another Orpheus to play music to thee,
   A Homer thy perfections all to sing.
I would be May, to clothe thee with its splendour,
   And Love itself adoring to caress thee ;
I'd call on fame, to speak my passion tender,
   I'd fain be the world's king, to serve and bless thee,
A sun to be thy light and thy defender,
   And heaven itself forever to possess thee.

                                Sir John Bowring.

TOME BURGUILLOS.

TO-MORROW AND TO-MORROW.

DREAMING of a to-morrow, which to-morrow
    Will be as distant then as 'tis to-day;
For Phœbus, who oft teases man with sorrow,
    Will never turn his car to light my way;
    So that I'm certain now *that* morning's ray
Will never dawn; and Phillis, thou may'st borrow
Some other phrase from language for to-morrow,
    To-morrow, and to-morrow, but betray!
I call'd upon Dan Cupid,—(when I find
    Sweet company, I never walk alone),
And said, Come with me, an' you are inclin'd;
    Let's seek this maiden morrow, for I groan
Impatient:—then I curse my eyes,—they're blind.
    Oh, no! I will not curse them,—they're my own.

Sir John Bowring.

MATEO VAZQUEZ DE LECA.

To Leander.

You were a foolish, though an amorous fellow,
Leander! had you for a boat but waited,
Death and the devil might have both been cheated,
And history have been spared the pains to tell how
A silly youth was drowned.—You might have gone
Dry-footed to your mistress—and have kissed her
In nuptial joy—but no!—for driven on
By an impatient passion's gust—you miss'd her,
And died.—A pity that!—in this our Seville,
You've not a notion how we cheat the devil;
And run no risk of colds, or disappointments:
True, love may graze us,—but the drowning plan
Is a mistake, which neither oil nor ointments,
Nor wit, nor wisdom, can get over, man.

Sir John Bowring.

FRANCISCO DE FIGUEROA.

ON THE DEATH OF GARCILASO DE LA VEGA, SLAIN IN BATTLE.

O BEAUTEOUS scion from the stateliest tree,
That e'er in fertile mead or forest grew !
With freshest bloom adorned and vigour new,
Gracious in form, and first in dignity !
   The same fell tempest, which by heaven's decree
Around thy parent stock resistless blew,
And far from Tejo fair its trunk o'erthrew.
In foreign clime hath stripped the leaves from thee.
   And the same pitying hand hath from the spot
Of cheerless ruin raised you to rejoice,
Where fruit immortal decks the withered stem !
   I will not, like the vulgar, mourn your lot ;
But, with pure incense and exulting voice,
Praise your high worth, and consecrate your fame.

Hon. William Herbert.

SANTA TERESA.

'Tis not thy terrors, Lord, thy dreadful frown,
That keep my step in duty's narrow path;
'Tis not the awful threatenings of Thy wrath,—
But that in virtue's sacred smile alone
I find or peace or happiness. Thy light,
In all its prodigality, is shed
Upon the worthy and the unworthy head;
And Thou dost wrap in misery's stormy night
The holy as the thankless. All is well;
Thy wisdom has to each his portion given;
Why should our hearts by selfishness be riven?
'Tis vain to murmur,—daring to rebel:
Lord, I would fear thee, though I feared not hell;
And love thee, though I had no hope of heaven.

Sir John Bowring.

QUEVEDO.

ROME.

AMID these scenes, O pilgrim, seek'st thou Rome?
Vain is thy search,—the pomp of Rome is fled!
Her silent Aventine is glory's tomb;—
Her walls, her shrines, but relics of the dead.
That hill, where Cæsars dwelt in other days,
Forsaken mourns, where once it towered sublime;
Each mouldering medal now far less displays
The triumphs won by Latium, than by Time.
Tiber alone survives;—the passing wave
That bathed her towers, now murmurs by her grave,
Wailing, with plaintive sounds, her fallen fanes.
Rome! of thine ancient grandeur all is past,
That seemed for years eternal framed to last;—
Nought but the wave, a fugitive, remains.

Felicia Hemans.

JUAN DE TARSIS.

TU, QUE LA DULCE VIDA EN TIERNAS ANOS.

Thou, who hast fled from life's enchanted bowers,
   In youth's gay spring, in beauty's glowing morn,
   Leaving thy bright array, thy path of flowers,
   For the rude convent-garb and couch of thorn;
Thou that, escaping from a world of cares,
   Hast found thy haven in devotion's fane,
   As to the port the fearful bark repairs
   To shun the midnight perils of the main—
Now the glad hymn, the strain of rapture pour,
   While on thy soul the beams of glory rise!
   For if the pilot hail the welcome shore
With shouts of triumph swelling to the skies,
   Oh! how shouldst thou the exulting pæan raise,
   Now heaven's bright harbour opens on thy gaze!

                                  Felicia Hemans.

CERVANTES.

THE AUTHOR TO HIS PEN.
(Introductory Sonnet to "Journey to Parnassus.")

To deck this frontispiece, since thou dost see
  No friend hath offered me a sonnet, none,
  Come thou, my ill-cut pen, and make me one,
If not so high flown as it ought to be;
From grave anxiety thou'lt set me free,
  I need not then through court and alley run
  To beg eulogiums; for I'd rather shun
Such vain and humbling search, I promise thee.
Let rhymes and sonnets go, for aught I care,
  To deck the door-posts of the upper few,
  Though flattery is at best but common stuff;
And grant me that this "Journey" have its share
  Of pungent salt, at least a pinch or two,
  I warrant thee 'twill sell; and so enough!

James Y. Gibson.

CERVANTES.

From *Don Quixote*.

In the dead silence of the peaceful night,
   When others' cares are hushed in soft repose,
   The sad account of my neglected woes
To conscious Heaven and Chloris I recite;
And when the sun, with his returning light,
   Forth from the east his radiant journey goes
   With accents such as sorrow only knows
My grief to tell is all my poor delight.
And when bright Phœbus from his starry throne
   Sends rays direct upon the parchèd soil,
Still in the mournful tale I persevere;
   Returning night renews my sorrow's toil;
And tho' from morn to night I weep and moan,
Nor Heaven nor Chloris doth my plainings hear.

Charles Jarvis.

CERVANTES.

From *Don Quixote*.

BELIEVE me, nymph, I feel th' impending blow,
   And glory in the near approach of death;
   For when thou see'st my corse devoid of breath,
My constancy and truth thou sure wilt know.
Welcome to me Oblivion's shade obscure!
   Welcome the loss of fortune, life, and fame!
   But thy loved features, and thy honoured name,
Deep graven on my heart, shall still endure.
And these, as sacred relics, will I keep
   Till that sad moment when to endless night
   My long-tormented soul shall take her flight.
Alas for him who on the darkened deep
   Floats idly, sport of the tempestuous tide,
   No port to shield him, and no star to guide.

Charles Jarvis.

CERVANTES.

LAST SONNET.

O POWERFUL, grand, thrice-blessed, and passing fair
   City of Rome! To thee I bend the knee,
   A pilgrim new, a lowly devotee,
Whose wonder grows to see thy beauty rare!
The sight of thee, past fame, beyond compare,
   Suspends the fancy, soaring tho' it be,
   Of him who comes to see and worship thee,
With naked feet, and tender loving care.
The soil of this thy land which now I view,
   Where blood of martyrs mingles with the clod,
   Is the world's relic, prized of every land;
No part of thee but serves as pattern true
   Of sanctity; as if the City of God
   Had been in every line its model grand!

James Y. Gibson.

LOPEZ MALDONADO.

The Brook.

LAUGH of the mountain !—lyre of bird and tree !
Pomp of the meadow ! mirror of the morn !
The soul of April, unto whom are born
The rose and jessamine, leaps wild in thee !
Although, where'er thy devious current strays,
The lap of earth with gold and silver teems,
To me thy clear proceeding brighter seems
Than golden sands that charm each shepherd's gaze.
How without guile thy bosom, all transparent
As the pure crystal, lets the curious eye
Thy secrets scan, thy smooth, round pebbles count !
How, without malice murmuring, glides thy current,
O sweet simplicity of days gone by !
Thou shun'st the haunts of man, to dwell in limpid fount !

Henry Wadsworth Longfellow.

LOPE DE VEGA.

TO-MORROW.

LORD, what am I, that, with unceasing care,
Thou didst seek after me,—that thou didst wait,
Wet with unhealthy dews, before my gate,
And pass the gloomy nights of winter there?
O strange delusion!—that I did not greet
Thy blest approach, and oh, to Heaven how lost,
If my ingratitude's unkindly frost
Has chilled the bleeding wounds upon thy feet.
How oft my guardian angel gently cried,
"Soul, from thy casement look, and thou shalt see
How He persists to knock and wait for thee!"
And oh! how often to that voice of sorrow
"To-morrow we will open," I replied,
And when the morrow came I answered still,
    "To-morrow."

Henry Wadsworth Longfellow.

LOPE DE VEGA.

The Good Shepherd.

Shepherd ! who with thine amorous, sylvan song
Hast broken the slumber that encompassed me,—
That mad'st thy crook from the accursèd tree,
On which thy powerful arms were stretched so long !
Lead me to mercy's ever-flowing fountains ;
For thou my shepherd, guard, and guide shalt be ;
I will obey thy voice, and wait to see
Thy feet all beautiful upon the mountains.
Hear, Shepherd !—Thou who for thy flock art dying,
O, wash away these scarlet sins, for thou
Rejoicest at the contrite sinner's vow.
O, wait !—to thee my weary soul is crying,—
Wait for me !—Yet why ask it when I see,
With feet nailed to the cross, thou'rt waiting still for me.

Henry Wadsworth Longfellow.

LOPE DE VEGA.

LA VIDA ES SUEÑO.

IF we're conceived in sin and born in pain;
   If life's a battle, and death ends the fray,
   And man becomes a clod, to worms a prey,
   After the worms but dust and air remain;
If nothing's left, and nothing's all his gain,
   Beauty a flower, ambition tyrant's sway,
   Glory and fame but empty thoughts alway,
   And every thought of intellect but vain;—
If but to drown why travel on this sea?
   Why should we pass our lives in endless strife?
   Why think of aught but how we may be free?
What use is honour or distinguished life,
   Or fame, when to Oblivion we must flee?
   Why build when Fate stands by with cruel knife?

Charles Tomlinson.

LOPE DE VEGA.

Not winter *crystal* ever was more clear
   That checks the current of the mountain stream ;
   Not high wrought *ebony* can blacker seem,
   Nor bluer doth the *flax* its blossom rear ;
Not yellower doth the eastern *gold* appear ;
   Nor purer can arise the scented steam
   Of *amber*, which luxurious men esteem ;
   Nor brighter scarlet doth the *sea-shell* bear ;
Than in the forehead, eye-brows, eyes, and hair,
   The breath, and lips, of my most beauteous queen,
   Are seen to dwell on earth, in face divine :—
And since like all together is my Fair,
   Lifeless elsewhere, alive in her are seen
   Ice, Ebony, Flax, Gold, Amber, and Carmine.

                Henry Richard, Lord Holland.

LOPE DE VEGA.

SONNET ON THE SONNET.

To write a sonnet doth Juana press me,
   I've never found me in such stress or pain ;
   A sonnet numbers fourteen lines, 'tis plain,
And three are gone, ere I can say, God bless me !
I thought that spinning rhymes might sore oppress me,
   Yet here I'm midway in the last quatrain ;
   And if the foremost tercet I can gain,
The quatrains need not any more distress me.
To the first tercet I have got at last,
   And travel through it with such right good will,
   That with this line I've finished it, I ween ;
I'm in the second now, and see how fast
   The thirteenth line runs tripping from my quill ;
   Hurrah, 'tis done !   Count if there be fourteen !

James Y. Gibson.

LUPERCIO LEONARDO.

TRUTH AND BEAUTY.

I MUST confess, Don John, on due inspection,
    That dame Elvira's charming red and white,
    Though fair they seem, are only hers by right
In that her money purchased their perfection;
But thou must grant as well, on calm reflection,
    That her sweet lie hath such a lustre bright,
    As fairly puts to shame the paler light,
And honest beauty of a true complexion!
And yet no wonder I distracted go
    With such deceit, when 'tis within our ken
    That Nature blinds us with ths self-same spell;
For that blue Heaven above, that charms us so,
    Is neither Heaven nor blue! Sad pity then,
    That so much Beauty is not Truth as well!

James Y. Gibson.

CALDERON.

From *El Principe Constante.*

THESE flowers, whose pomp was joyous to behold,
    When the white dawn awoke them out of sleep,
    At eve shall be a ruin fit to weep,
Lulled in the darkling night's embraces cold.
This posy bright with listed hues of gold,
    Snow-white and purple, rivalling heaven's bow,
    Will be a warning to our life below;
So doth one day its little life enfold.

To flower, the rose displayed her buds at morn,
    And to grow old and wither, did she flower;
One is her cradle and her grave forlorn.
    So men behold brief fortune's earthly dower,
To die upon the day when they were born,
    For the past ages are but as an hour.

Arthur Platt.

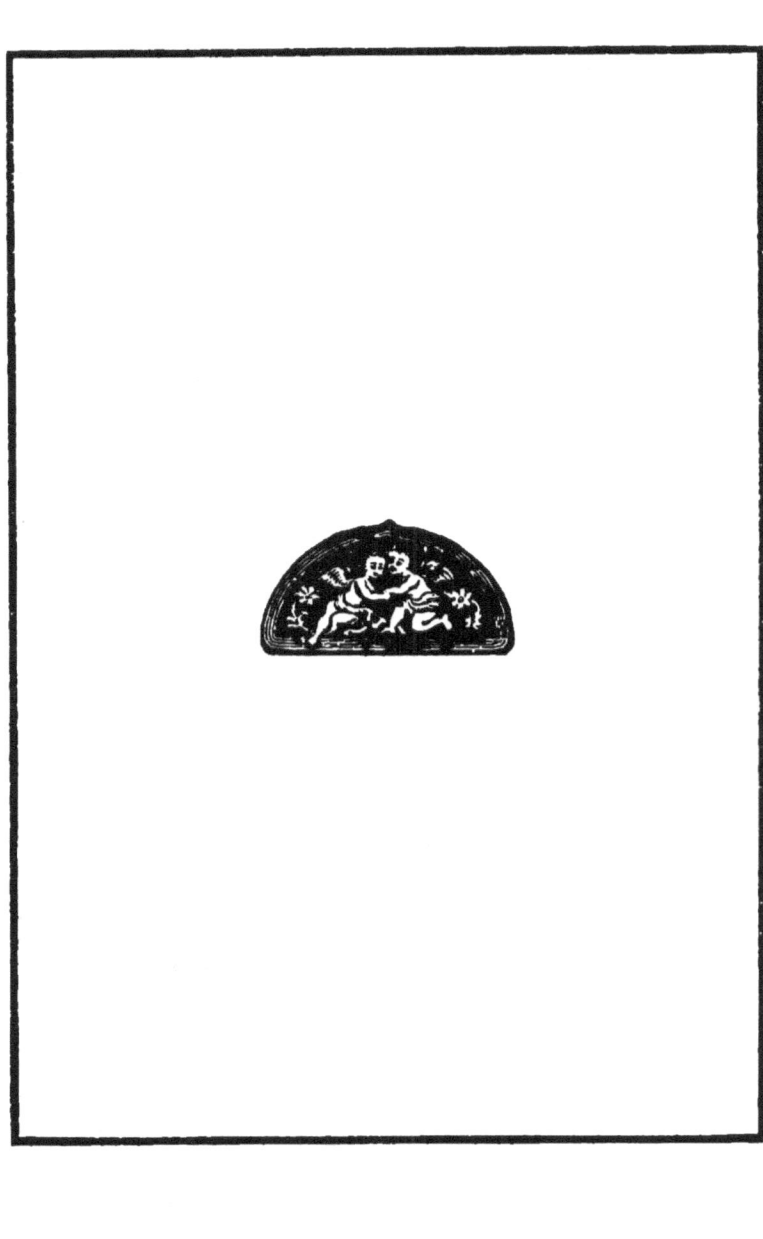

Portuguese Sonnets.

PORTUGUESE SONNETS.

CAMOENS.

An Adieu to Tagus.

Waters of gentle Tagus, calmly flowing
Through these green fields ye freshen as ye flow,
On flocks and herds, plants, flowers, all things that grow,
On shepherds and on nymphs delight bestowing;
I know not, ah! sweet streams, despair of knowing
When I shall come again; for as I go,
And ponder why, ye fill me with such woe,
That in my heart a deep distrust is growing.
The Fates have e'en decreed this sad adieu,
Aiming to change my joys into despair,
This sad adieu that weighs upon my years:
Of them complaining, yearning after you,
With sighs I shall invade some distant air,
And trouble other waters with my tears.

J. J. Aubertin.

CAMOENS.

ON THE DEATH OF KING SEBASTIAN.

His generous visage gashed with heathen blade,
His Royal brow with dust and blood all wan,
Came to the mournful boat of Acheron
The great Sebastian, past into a shade.
The cruel boatman, seeing that undismayed
The King perforce would cross, pronounced his ban,
Vowing that never o'er that stream was man
Ferried, whose funeral rites were still unpaid.
The valorous King, whose anger knew no bounds,
Replied, Oh! false old man, and dost not know
Others by force of gold have passed before?
What! of a king all bathed in blood of Moor
Darest thou to claim that he a tomb shall show?
Claim it of him who comes with fewer wounds.

J. J. Aubertin.

CAMOENS.

TO A FILLET, GIVEN HIM IN JEST, FROM HER HAIR, BY A LADY WITH WHOM HE WAS IN LOVE.

SWEET, delicate fillet, who art left behind,
In pledge the joy I merit to redeem,
If, only seeing thee, half lost I seem,
What with the locks round which thou erst didst wind?
Those golden tresses where thou wast entwined,
That hold the sunbeam's glow in light esteem,
I know not if to mock my prayerful dream,
Or if to bind me thou didst them unbind.
Sweet fillet, in my hands I see thee lie,
And that my grief some solace I may show,
As one who hath no other, thee I take :
And if my wish thou dost not satisfy,
Still, in the rule of love, I'll bid her know,
Sometimes we keep the part for the whole's sake.

J. J. Aubertin.

CAMOENS.

SIBELLA.

WITHIN a wood nymphs were inhabiting,
Sibella, lovely nymph, was wandering free ;
And climbing up into a shady tree,
The yellow blossoms there was gathering.
Cupid, who thither ever turned his wing,
Cool in his shady mid-day sleep to be,
Would on a branch, e'er sleeping, pendent see
The bow and arrows he was wont to bring.
The nymph, who now the moment fitting saw
For so great enterprise, in nought delays,
But flies the scorner with the arms she ta'en.
She bears the arrows in her eyes, to draw.
Oh ! shepherds fly, for every one she slays,
Save me alone, who live by being slain.

J. J. Aubertin.

CAMOENS.

Se a ninguem tratais com desamor.

If thou indifference wilt display to none,
Rather towards every one endearing art,
If thou towards every one dost show a heart,
That fullest love and gentleness doth own,
Henceforth towards me be thy disfavour shown;
In odious scorn or coldness stand apart;
There shall I come to think, beneath the smart,
Thou showest favour unto me alone.
For if to all so tender thou wilt prove,
'Tis clear the only favoured one is he
Towards whom thine eye doth with displeasure move.
Scarcely, indeed, can I be loved by thee,
If in thy heart thou hast another love,
For Love is one, nor can divided be.

J. J. Aubertin.

CAMOENS.

CORYDON AND TITYRUS.

BENEATH a green and lofty oak reclined,
Corydon o'er the scale his finger threw
In ivy's shade, whose clinging tendrils grew
Among the trees, and round the branches twined.
Of Amaryllis, nymph for whom he pined,
He sang the loves, love's moving power he knew;
The birds among the branches listening flew,
And lower down did stream of crystal wind.
To him comes Tityrus, who idly roved,
Driving his meagre cattle o'er the plain;
Tityrus was friend of Corydon best loved.
He tells him all his torment and his pain;
By other's speech the embittered is not moved.
Nor grief makes sorrowful the heart that's fain.

J. J. Aubertin.

CAMOENS.

THE FISHER IONIO CALLS ON THE WAVES TO RESTORE TO HIM HIS DROWNED LOVE.

ALL hushed the heaven and earth, and wind the same,
The waves all spreading o'er the sandy plain,
While sleep doth in the sea the fish enchain,
Nocturnal silence brooding as a dream;—
Prostrate with love, Ionio, fisher, came
Where the breeze moved the waters of the main;
Weeping, the well-loved name he called in vain,
That can no more be called but as a name;
Oh! waves, or ere love slay me, thus he cried,
Restore to me my nymph who, ah! so soon,
Ye taught my soul was subject to the grave.
No one replies; from far beats ocean's tide;
All softly moves the grove; and the wind's moan
Bears off the voice that to the wind he gave.

J. J. Aubertin.

CAMOENS.

THE SHEPHERDESS NISE.

AURORA with her new-born crystal ray
Arose the enamelled world again to dress,
When Nise, fair and gentle shepherdess,
Departed whence her only true life lay.
The light of eyes that darkened those of day
She raised, while flowing anxious tears oppress,
Of self, fate, time, all wearied to distress,
And gazing heavenward thus did pensive say:
Rise, tranquil sun, once more all pure and shining,
Clear purple morn with new-born light be clad,
And see sad souls with you their grief resigning;
But my poor soul, while others all are glad,
Ye know ye ne'er shall see but as repining,
Nor any other shepherdess so sad.

J. J. Aubertin.

CAMOENS.

Audaces Fortuna Juvat.

Never did love his boldness hurtful find ;
Fortune hath ever favours for the bold ;
For cowardice, that shivers in the cold,
Hangs like a stone on freedom of the mind.
Who dares the Firmament sublime ascend,
Meets there a star, whereby his course is told ;
The good mere fancy in its range doth hold
Illusive is, soon scattered by the wind.
A path for fortune should be opened free ;
To none, without himself, will greatness fall ;
Chance moving only in first steps appears.
To dare is valour, madness 'twill not be ;
He to whom fortune shows thee, loses all,
If, coward like, he doth not scorn his fears.

J. J. Aubertin.

CAMOENS.

On seeing Catharina de Athaide in Church and losing his heart.

The souls of all were sad in solemn prayer,
Owning the mercy of their Lord Divine,
While in His holy presence so benign,
The tribute that was due they offered there:
My heart till then was free from every care,
Till then my fate had traced an equal line,
When lo! some eyes, too high and pure for mine,
Assaulted all my reason, unaware.
The novel vision struck me wholly blind;
From strangeness sprang the magic charm displayed
By that soft presence, all angelical.
And can I no alleviation find?
Oh! why in births hath Human Nature made
Difference so great, and we her children all!

J. J. Aubertin.

CAMOENS.

ON THE DEATH OF DONNA CATHARINA DE ATHAIDE.

My gentle spirit ! thou who hast departed
So early, of this life in discontent,
Rest thou there ever, in Heaven's firmament,
While I live here on earth all broken-hearted ;
In that Ethereal Seat, where thou didst rise,
If memory of this life so far consent,
Forget not thou my ardent love unspent,
Which thou didst read so perfect in mine eyes.
And if, perchance, aught worthy there appears
In my great cureless anguish for thy death,
Oh ! pray to God who closed so soon thy years,
That He will also close my sorrowing breath,
And swiftly call me hence thy form to see,
As swiftly he deprived these eyes of thee.

J. J. Aubertin.

CAMOENS.

The eyes where love in chastest fire would glow,
Joying to be consumed amidst their light,
The face whereon with wondrous lustre bright
The purple rose was blushing o'er the snow;
The hair whereof the sun would envious grow,
It made his own less golden to the sight;
The well-formed body and the hand so white,
All to cold earth reduced lies here below!
In tender age, a beauty all entire,
E'en like a blossom gathered ere its time,
Lies withered in the hand of heartless death:
How doth not Love for pity's sake expire?
Ah! not for her who flies to life sublime,
But for himself whom night extinguisheth.

J. J. Aubertin.

CAMOENS.

Beholding Her.

When I behold you, Lady! when my eyes
Dwell on the deep enjoyment of your sight,
I give my spirit to that one delight,
And earth appears to me a Paradise.
And when I hear you speak, and see you smile,
Full satisfied, absorb'd, my center'd mind
Deems all the world's vain hopes and joys the while
As empty as the unsubstantial wind.
Lady! I feel your charms, yet dare not raise
To that high theme the unequal song of praise,—
A power for that to language was not given;
Nor marvel I, when I those beauties view,
Lady! that He, whose power created you,
Could form the stars and yonder glorious heaven.

Robert Southey.

CAMOENS.

HIS INSUFFICIENCY OF PRAISE.

So sweet the lyre, so musical the strain,
By which my suit, Belovëd! is expressed,
That, hearing them, no such indifferent breast
But welcomes Love and his delicious pain,
And opes to his innumerable train
Of sweet persuasions, lovely mysteries,
Brief angers, gentle reconcilements, sighs
And ardour unabash'd by proud disdain.
Yet, when I strive to sing what beauty dwells
Upon thy brow, so oft in scorn array'd,
My song upon the unworthy lips expires.
It must be loftier verse than mine that tells
Of loveliness like thine. My Muse, dismay'd,
Folds her weak wing and silently retires.

Richard Garnett.

JOAŌ XAVIER DE MATOS.

NIGHT-FALL.

THE sun has set, with duskiest shades imbued
   The lingering daylight slowly dies away,
   And Night's dark fingers have already strewed
   The air with cheerless clouds, opaque and gray;
And scarce discern I where my cottage stands,
   And scarce the beech from rueful cypress know;
   'Tis silence all, save that upon the sands
   The distant waters moan and murmur low.
Languid I scan the wastes of dreary air,
   A deadly grief sits heavy on my soul,
   Unbidden tears hang quivering in my eyes,
And I could pray, if I might breathe a prayer,
   That night's dull car might never cease to roll,
   And sunbeam never more illume the skies.

Richard Garnett.

RODRIGUEZ LOBO.

Past Joys.

Dear Tagus, what immeasurable space
   Our present from our former lot divides!
   Glassy of yore, now turbid are thy tides,
   Once smiles my brow adorned, now tears deface.
Thy change is work of tempests, whose descent
   Robs thy clear current of its silvery sheen,
   Mine of the brilliant eyes and sovran mien
   That portion me my bliss or discontent.
As we are thus participant in woe,
   Would we were so in all things; and, as pain,
   So simultaneous joy might feel! But no!
Flower-fostering Spring shall look and see no stain
   In thy clear mirror; but I cannot know
   If my lost bliss will ever come again.

Richard Garnett.

FRANCISCO DE ALDANA.

THE NATIVE LAND.

CLEAR fount of light ! my native land on high
Bright with a glory that shall never fade !
Mansion of truth ! without a veil or shade,
Thy holy quiet meets the spirit's eye.
There dwells the soul in its ethereal essence,
Gasping no longer for life's feeble breath ;
But sentinelled in heaven, its glorious presence
With pitying eye beholds, yet fears not, death.
Belovëd country ! banished from thy shore,
A stranger in this prison-house of clay,
The exiled spirit weeps and sighs for thee !
Heavenward the bright perfections I adore
Direct, and the sure promise cheers the way,
That, whither love aspires, there shall my dwelling be.

Henry Wadsworth Longfellow.

FRANCISCO DE ALDANA.

The Image of God.

O Lord ! that seest, from yon starry height,
   Centred in one the future and the past,
   Fashioned in thine own image, see how fast
   The world obscures in me what once was bright !
Eternal Sun ! the warmth which thou hast given
   To cheer life's flowery April, fast decays ;
   Yet, in the hoary winter of my days,
   For ever green shall be my trust in Heaven.
Celestial King ! O let thy presence pass
   Before my spirit, and an image fair
   Shall meet that look of mercy from on high,
As the reflected image in a glass
   Doth meet the look of him who seeks it there,
   And owes its being to the gazer's eye.

Henry Wadsworth Longfellow.

CURVO SEMEDO.

"It is a fearful night ; a feeble glare
    Streams from the sick moon in the o'erclouded sky ;
    The ridgy billows, with a mighty cry,
    Rush on the foamy beaches wild and bare ;
No bark the madness of the waves will dare ;
    The sailors sleep ; the winds are loud and high ;
    Ah, peerless Laura ! for whose love I die,
    Who gazes on thy smiles while I despair?"—
As thus, in bitterness of heart, I cried,
    I turned, and saw my Laura, kind and bright,
    A messenger of gladness, at my side ;
To my poor bark she sprang with footstep light ;
    And as we furrowed Tejo's heaving tide,
    I never saw so beautiful a night.

William Cullen Bryant.

BOCCAGE

On Nelson.

ENTERING Elysium, diademed with light,
   Nelson, in blood-stained robe, behold appear !
   The shades are stricken with unwonted fear,
And round him crowd the ghosts of men of might.
Cries Alexander, rivetting his sight,
   "What lustrous mortal thou, that enterest here?"
   "'Tis I who raised from thraldom to her sphere
Europe, bowed down, half captive from the fight.
Incarnadined with blood I left the wave,
   A bolt upon the furious Gaul I threw,
My country raises trophies o'er my grave."—
   On this the Macedonian weeps anew ;
He to whom Victory vast regions gave,
   Envies the man who did one race subdue.

J. J. Aubertin.

Swedish Sonnets.

SWEDISH SONNETS.

GUSTAV ROSENHANE.

I.

Deep in a vale where rocks on every side
   Shut out the winds, and scarcely let the sun
   Between them dart his rays down one by one,
Where all was still and cool in summer-tide,
And softly, with her whispering waves that sighed,
   A little river, that had scarce begun
   Her silver course, made bold to fleet and run
Down leafy falls to woodlands dense and wide,
There stood a tiny plain, just large enow
   To give small mountain-folk right room to dance,
   With oaks and limes and maples ringed around;
Hither I came, and viewed its turf askance,
   Its solitude with beauty seemed a-glow,—
   My Love had walked there and 'twas holy ground !

Edmund Gosse.

GUSTAV ROSENHANE.

II.

AND then I sat me down, and gave the rein
   To my wild thoughts, till many a song that rang
   From boughs around where hidden warblers sang
Recalled me from myself; then "Oh! in vain"
I said, "do these outpour the tender strain?
   Can these sweet birds that with such airs harangue
   Their feathered loves, like me, feel sorrow's pang?
Ah! would that I, like them, had pinions twain!
Straight would I fly to her whom I love best,
   Nor vainly warbling in the woodland sing,
But chirp my prayer, and preen my plumèd crest,
   And to this spot once more her beauty bring,
   And flutter round her flight with supple wing,
And lead her to my secret leafy nest."

Edmund Gosse.

OLOF WEXIONIUS.

On the Death of a Pious Lady.

The earthly roses at God's call have made
  Way, lady, for a dress of heavenly white,
  In which thou walk'st with other figures bright,
Once loved on earth, who now, like thee arrayed,
Feast on two-fold ambrosia, wine and bread;
  They lead thee up by sinuous paths of light
  Through lilied fields that sparkle in God's sight,
And crown thee with delights that never fade.
O thou thrice-sainted mother, in that bliss,
Forget not thy two daughters, whom a kiss
  At parting left as sad as thou art glad;
In thy deep joy think how for thee they weep,
Or conjure through the shifting glass of sleep
  The saint heaven hath, the mother once they had.

Edmund Gosse.

STAGNELIUS.

Hope Repulsed.

Up through the ruins of my earthly dreams
   I catch the stars of immortality;
   What store of joy can hide in heaven for me?
What other hope feed those celestial gleams?
Can there be other grapes whose nectar streams
   For me, whom earth's vine fails? oh! can it be
   That this abandoned heart again may see
A forehead garlanded, an eye that beams?
Alas! 'tis childhood's dream that vanisheth!
   The heaven-born soul that feigns it can return,
   And end in peace this hopeless strife with fate!
There is no backward step; 'tis only death
   Can quench at last these wasting fires that burn,
   Can break the chain, the captive liberate.

Edmund Gosse.

STAGNELIUS.

LUNA.

Deep slumber hung o'er sea and hill and plain ;
   With pale pink cheek fresh from her watery caves
   Slow rose the Moon out of the midnight waves ;
Like Venus out of ocean born again,
Olympian blazed she on the dark blue main ;
   " So shall, ye Gods !" hark how my weak hope raves !
   " My happy star ascend the sea that laves
Its shores with grief, and silence all my pain ! "
With that there sighed a wandering midnight breeze,
High up among the topmost tufted trees,
   And o'er the moon's face blew a veil of cloud ;
And in the breeze my genius spake, and said,
" While thy heart stirs, thy glimmering hope has fled,
   And like the moon lies muffled in a shroud."

Edmund Gosse.

STAGNELIUS.

MEMORY.

O CAMP of flowers, with poplars girdled round,
   Grey guardians of life's soft and purple bud!
   O silver spring, beside whose brimming flood
My pensive childhood its Elysium found!
O happy hours by love and fancy crowned,
   Whose horn of plenty flatteringly subdued
   My heart into a trance, whence, with a rude
And horrid blast, fate came my soul to hound!
Who was the goddess that empowered you all
   Thus to bewitch me? Out of wasting snow
   And lily-leaves her head-dress should be made!
Weep, my poor lute! nor on Astræa call,
   She will not smile, nor I, who mourn below,
   Till I, a shade in heaven, clasp her, a shade.

Edmund Gosse.

Polish Sonnets.

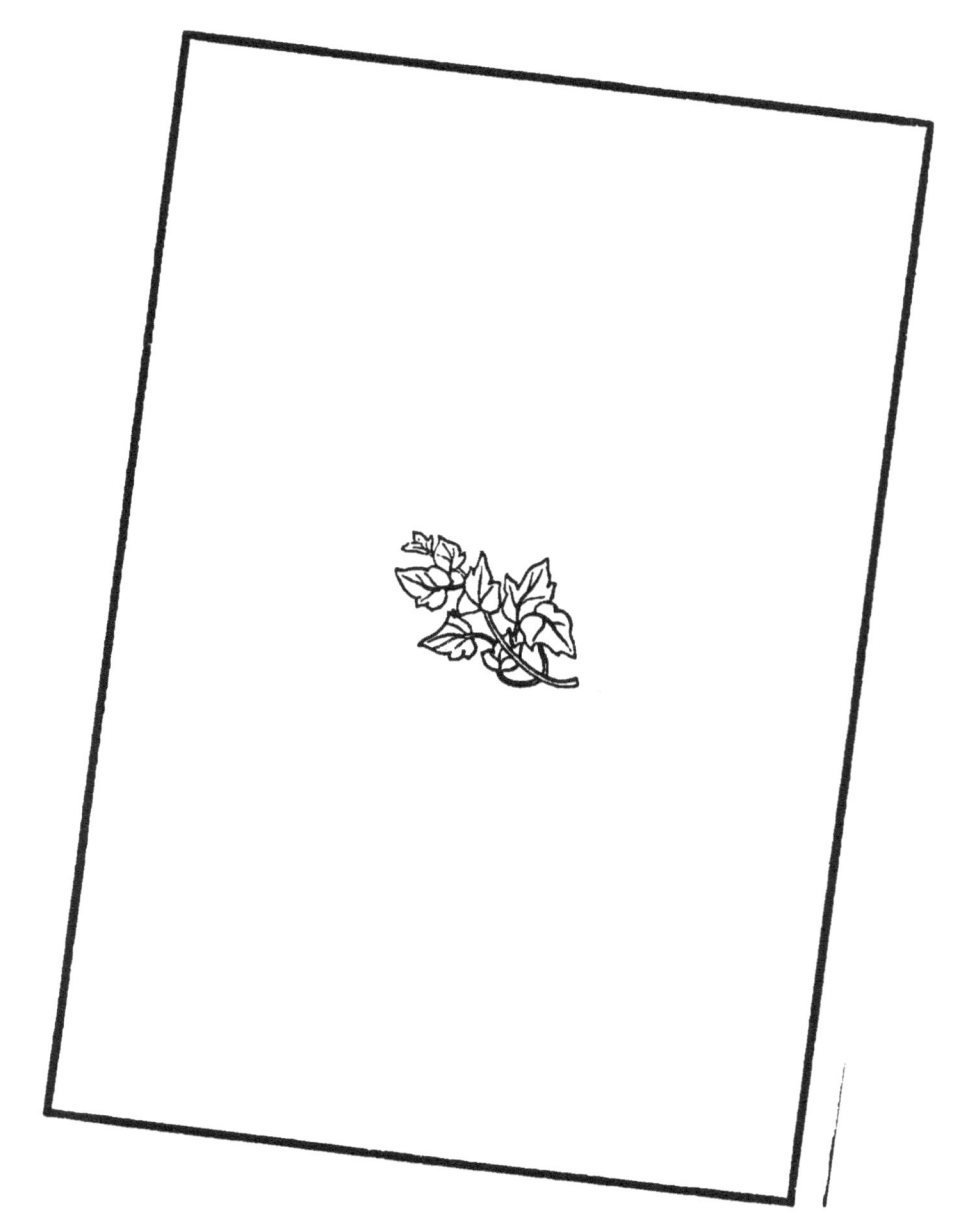

POLISH SONNETS.

MICKIEWICZ.

The Rock of Aiudah.

Aiudah ! See the blackening waves advance
   Against the shore, like armies to the fray,
Then break in silvery clouds, while rainbows dance
   In the long lines of diamonded spray !

They strike, they break, they die on the lagoon
   Like stranded whales, their long triumphant swell
Now hides the prostrate shore, retreating soon
   They leave the pearl, the coral, and the shell.

So, youthful bard, will Passion's surges roll
   On thy young heart, but do thou seize the lyre
   And wake the soul of music, at her hymn
The threatening floods will suddenly retire,
   And on the strand of thy delivered soul
   Leave songs whose splendours never shall be dim.

Richard Garnett.

MICKIEWICZ.

Eastward, the sun arises clad in gold,
    Westward, the waning moonbeam disappears;
Like spreading fires the rose's buds unfold,
    The violet droops, borne down by dewy tears.

My Laura, from her casement, bright and glad,
    Shines forth upon me, on my knees I bow;
Winding her golden tresses, *Why so sad*
    The moon, she asks, *the violet, and thou?*

'Tis eve, how changed! with added glory burns
    The orient moon, and, now no more forlorn,
    The violet drinks the sweet reviving breeze;
And Laura to her oriel returns
    In lovelier garb, with dearer charms, and sees
    Me sad as erst she saw me in the morn.

Richard Garnett.

Modern Greek Sonnets.

GREEK SONNETS.

ARISTOMENÊS PROVILEGIOS.

Ah! now, at last, I freely breathe to-day.
  The pain, and all the gnawing and unrest,
  Which so long wrestling with did weight my breast,
Are over. Conquered Love hath flown away.

O blissful calm! I hail thee with thy train
  Of many angels 'round thee fair and bright;
  My spirit walks forgetful, to the light
Of the blue ether rising once again.

Now heal'd—as if so pitiful a wound
It ne'er had known, my heart doth gaily bound,
And seeks—its past commotions to renew.

As when the sailor—saved, though tempest tost,
Through the fierce wintry winds so nearly lost—
Longs his drear wanderings to commence anew.

E. Mayhew Edmonds.

ALEX. R. RHANGABE.

Love.

Behold, sweet love, all things on this our earth
   Have been prepared with leavening of tears !
   With tears, delight—with tears, renown appears,—
With mingled tears hath every joy its birth.

O'er land and sea Man passes, still at strife ;
   He passes—memories, footprints, leaving none ,
   With tears mute science following alone,
Grows old—and dies—ere he hath studied Life.

His vague desires across black chaos sail,
He hopes—his hopes untimely withering fail.
Winged shadows he pursues,—on, on, they move.

Yet creeping through the darkness gently gleams
For him th' illumining light of one star's beams ;
One smile alone—one smile—consoles him—Love.

                  E. Mayhew Edmonds.

Dutch Sonnets.

DUTCH SONNETS.

PIETER CORNELISZOON HOOFT.

To Hugo Grotius.

GREAT soul, that with the keenness of clear sight
  Just measure takest of approaching things,
  Yet by the wisdom that high memory brings
Dost hold full judgment of all past years' flight,
What God or man in counsel or of right
  May speak, thou can'st expound; from thee light
    springs;
  Thou art the eye of Holland; when storm rings
In starless weather, thou dost lift thy light.
Sun of our sphere, how shall I liken you?
Art thou a blast that God from heaven out-blew,
  Come to our hearts, to find them well prepared?
Or, from the roofs of paradise, a spirit,
Dowered with all skill that sons of light inherit,
  Whose wit and power our earth with heaven hath
    shared?

Edmund Gosse.

Sept. 3, 1616.

PIETER CORNELISZOON HOOFT.

FRIENDSHIP.

THIS earth, embossed with mountains, laced with streams,
  Starred with fair cities ringed about with towers,
Whose face with hill and laughing valley gleams,
  Whose shadowy woods are full of tender flowers,
The birds, the careless beasts beneath the moon,
  And that conceited race of feeble man,
All hold their place by harmony, and soon
  Sans friendship would sink out of nature's plan.
From manly friendship cities take their root,
  Their nurture and their life; from strife their death;
  Thro' civil jars they pant with heavy breath;
    So dangerous is division in the State!
In harmony the seeds of glory shoot,
    And peace at home makes little kingdoms great.

Edmund Gosse.

JAN VAN BROEKHUIZEN.

BEYOND the Rhine, in solitude and snows,
    Through every starless night and cheerless day,
    I muse, and waste myself in thought away,
    And breathe my sighs to where the Amstel flows.
My spring of life is hastening to its close,
    The sun of youth emits its latest ray,
    While grief asserts its most ungentle sway;
    And toils I bear, but toils without repose.
But, oh, my past enjoyment, life, and light!
    How soon should sorrow take its hurried flight,
    And every thought that pains my breast depart,
If thou wert present when my spirits pine!
    For thou wouldst bring, with those sweet eyes of thine,
    A summer in the land,—a heaven within my heart.

Sir John Bowring.

LATIN SONNET.

HUGO GROTIUS.

To Thomas Farnabie.
(On Editing the Tragedies of Seneca.)

Life's mirror, and our teacher, is the Stage,—
   And to the Stage life the Tragedian gives;
   Throned 'mid tragedians Seneca still lives,
   And *thou*, whose light here gleams upon his page:
Each star pre-eminent, each classic sage,
   That shines supreme, from thee his light derives;
   By thee restored the Tragic Muse revives,
Whence may thy praise be sung from age to age.

Nor Leyden nor let London claim, entailed
   For their sole heritage, thy treasured store,—
   Whiche'er thou choosest as thy home to be,—
But read in every town for evermore,
   By sland'rous tongues untouched, by none assailed,
   May Time's dread tyranny now yield to thee.

                    Samuel Waddington.

Notes.

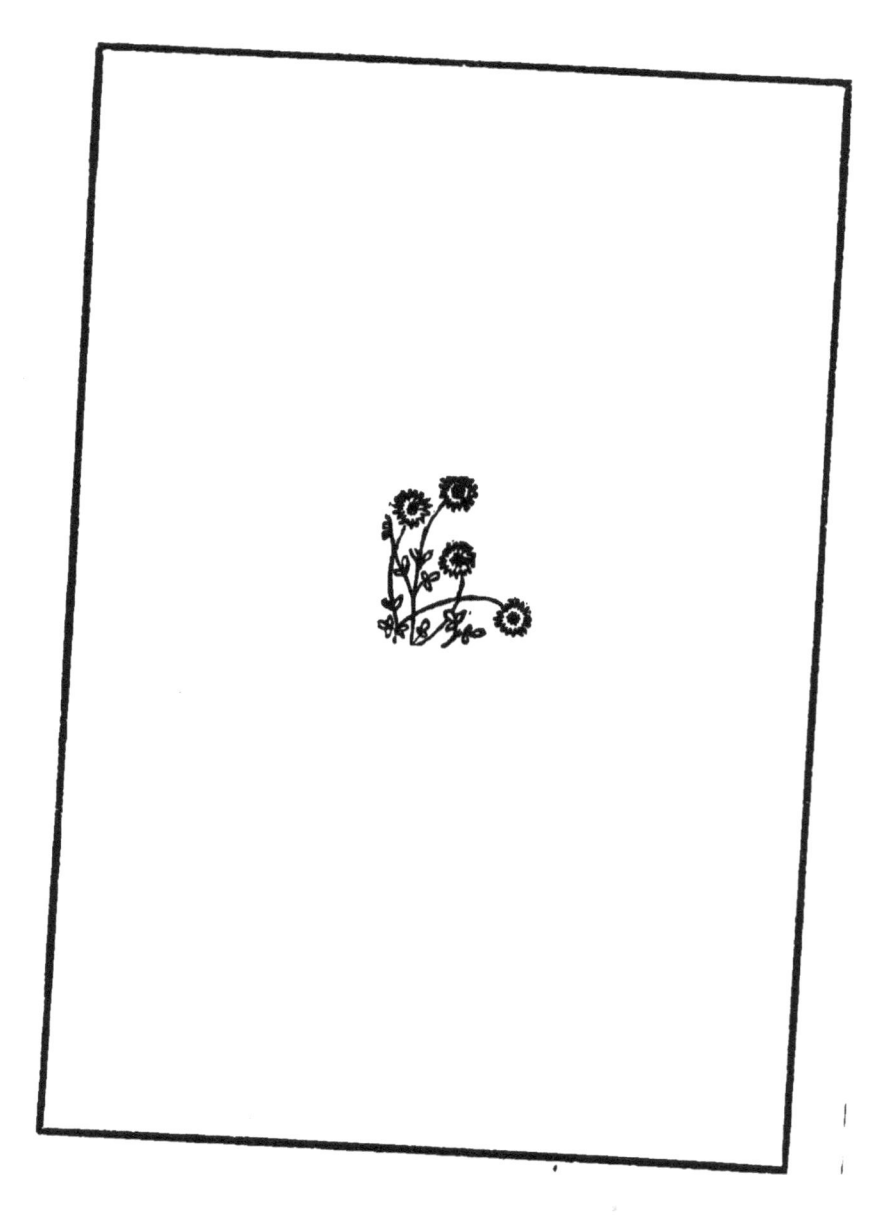

NOTES.

Page 1.— Fra Guittone D'Arezzo, who flourished about 1250 A.D., belonged to the religious and military order of *Cavalieri di Santa Maria;* and Rossetti, in his *Dante and his Circle*, observes that Guittone seems to have enjoyed a greater literary reputation than almost any writer of his day. He also points out that the sonnet by Guittone to "The Virgin" is somewhat remarkable from Petrarch's having transplanted its last line into his *Trionfi d' Amore*. Guittone wrote more than two hundred sonnets; and although Lodovico Vernaccia and Piero delle Vigne preceded him in the composition of this form of verse, yet the number of sonnets they have left us is so small, as compared with those by Guittone, that we are justified in considering him the first principal writer of the "Sonnet."

Page 2.—Guido Guinicelli, of Bologna, also flourished about the middle of the thirteenth century. His sonnets have the charm of the most graceful and mellifluous verse, and he is justly regarded as the best of the Italian poets that preceded Dante, by whom he is very highly praised.

Page 6.—This translation of Bonaggiunta's sonnet on "the danger of falling *out of* love" is taken from the

Notes to Dante's *Divine Comedy*, translated by C. B. Cayley. Bonaggiunta (Buonagiunta) was a native of Lucca, and appears to have been a poet and orator of considerable repute. He is depicted in the twenty-fourth Canto of the *Purgatorio* as undergoing torment amongst the Gluttons, and is said to have been intimate with Dante, and to have carried on a poetical correspondence with him. Evidently Dante did not forget his old friends.

Benvenuto observes:—" Buonagiunta, of Urbisani, an honourable man of the city of Lucca, a brilliant orator in his mother tongue, a facile producer of rhymes, and still more facile consumer of wines; who knew our author (Dante) in his lifetime, and sometimes corresponded with him."

Page 7.—

" Vanna and Bice and my gentle love."

Respecting this line Mr. W. M. Rossetti writes—"Shelley has fallen into a singular misapprehension here. Bice is simply Beatrice, and is herself, of course, Dante's 'gentle love.' The literal translation of the Italian runs—' And then Lady Vanna and Lady Bice, with her who is on number thirty.' The latter enigmatic-sounding phrase (not enigmatic to a Dantesque reader) indicates the inamorata of Lapo Gianni. If we were to read, 'and *his* gentle love,' the sense would be correct; and possibly *my* is, after all, only a misprint."

This sonnet has also been translated by Hayley, and by D. G. Rossetti.

Page 14.—The editor has to thank Mr. Brander Matthews for calling his attention to this beautiful translation by Dr. Parsons of what is by many regarded as the finest of Dante's sonnets.

NOTES. 247

Here is another excellent rendering of the same sonnet by Mr. C. Kegan Paul:—

" So gentle, honester than others are
My lady seems, if any she salute,
That every tongue grows tremulously mute,
Nor any eye to look on her may dare.
Though of her praises she is all aware,
Kindly she goes, humility her suit,
And seems as though she were an heavenly fruit
Dropt upon earth miraculously rare;
And as we look entranced, from out her eye
There goes a pleasing sweetness through the heart,
Which none who see her ever fail to prove;
A phantom sweet, instinct with only love,
She seems if ever her sweet lips she part,
Who to the spirit says in passing ' sigh.' "

The following is a translation I have myself attempted of another of Dante's sonnets, entitled "Beauty and Duty":—

" Lo, throned upon my spirit's loftiest height,
  Here of true love discourse fair ladies twain;
  And one, with honoured prudence in her train,
  In valorous courtesy is richly dight:—
The other glistens with the golden light
  Of smiles and winning grace, where beauties reign;
  And I, of each enamoured, still remain
  The slave of each, as Love asserts his might.
Beauty and Duty, these my spirit woo,
  And urge their suit, doubting if loyal kiss
  To *both* can e'er be given, and faithful prove:
Yet saith the fount of gentle speech and true,—
  Both may be thine!—Beauty, for dearest bliss;
  But Duty, for good deeds, shall win thy love."

The first eight lines of D. G. Rossetti's translation of this sonnet are as follows:—

> "Two ladies to the summit of my mind
> Have clomb, to hold an argument of love ;
> The one has wisdom with her from above,
> For every noblest virtue well design'd ;
> The other beauty's tempting power refined
> And the high charm of perfect grace approve :
> And I, as my sweet Master's will doth move,
> At feet of both their favours am reclined."

The expression, "the summit of my mind," may, perhaps, appear to some to be rather prosaic, but Rossetti seems to have taken it from Lyell's blank-verse rendering of this sonnet, published nearly fifty years ago, beginning—

> "Two ladies on the summit of my mind
> Their station take, to hold discourse of love."

Mr. Lyell was a friend, it will be remembered, of Rossetti's father. The third and fourth lines of this sonnet in the original are—

> "L'una ha in sè cortesia e valore,
> Prudenzia ed onestate 'n compagnia."

None of Rossetti's translations have been included in this volume, as the permission of the publishers could not be obtained.

Mr. William Davies writes respecting these compositions by Dante:—"His sonnets steal over the soul like a breath of summer wind, making it sigh for pure joy of its sweetness—a sweetness so refreshing, and so delicate, that one wishes it might never die, but go on whispering its delicious music for ever. Every

word is a breathing vitality; the utmost simplicity of expression being united to the greatest profundity of conception. They have an inevitable ease constituting the most lucid transparency of style, which makes all shade of Confusion fly before it as from the rod of the angel of Order. They seem born out of the soul as naturally as flowers out of the earth, and are as lovely and as welcome; apparently fragile as a gossamer any wind might blow away, yet strong enough to withstand the tempest, and take its rude airs with soft odours, allaying its boisterous disorders with the tender submissiveness of interior calm."
—(*Quarterly Review*, January 1873.)

Page 31.—These two translations by Lady Dacre are taken from the *Essays on Petrarch* by Ugo Foscolo, who in his dedication writes—"I am prompted to inscribe these pages with your ladyship's name, as well by my own gratitude, as by the opinion of those distinguished literary characters, whose kind assistance, surpassed only by yours, has enabled me to present my Essays to the English reader. With one voice and with national pride they pronounce, that your poetry has preserved the very spirit of Petrarch with a fidelity hardly to be hoped for, and certainly unattained by any other translation." Without questioning the correctness of these observations by Ugo Foscolo, which were written in January 1823, during his residence at South Bank, Regent's Park, I would add that, so far as my own taste and judgment are concerned, there are few, if any, translations of Petrarch's sonnets more graceful, and in every respect satisfactory, than those by Colonel Higginson, of which six are included in this selection. I have to thank him very heartily for sending me from America his volume entitled *Old Port Days*, from which they are quoted.

The translators of Petrarch, whose name is legion, would hardly enable us to credit Filippo Villani when he writes, that "the musical modulation of the verses which Petrarch addressed to Laura flowed so melodiously that even the most grave could not refrain from repeating them." But the fault in this matter is with the translators, and not with the poet. "His style," observes Longfellow, "was melodious and polished to the last degree of elaborate finish of which expression is capable." And his manuscripts which still exist show that he spared no pains in the correction of his work. It is to be regretted, perhaps, that he did not choose other subjects for his verse besides the one monotonous theme of his love for Laura. At the head of one of his sonnets he writes in Latin, "I began this by the impulse of the Lord (Domino jubente), 10th September, at the dawn of day, after my morning prayers,"—and one cannot but wish that he had sometimes been impelled to write on other subjects more worthy of his genius.

Page 40.—The following translation by Mr. Francis Hueffer of a sonnet addressed to Petrarch after his death by Boccaccio has been kindly forwarded to me by Mr. W. M. Rossetti. It unfortunately reached me too late for insertion amongst the Italian Sonnets in the foregoing selection.

SONNET ADDRESSED TO PETRARCH AFTER HIS DEATH, BY BOCCACCIO.

> Now has thou left me, master dear, now art
> At rest in that eternal house, where free
> From earthly strife God-chosen souls shall be
> When from this sinful world they do depart.

>   Now art thou, where full many a time thy heart
>   Drew thee thy Laura once again to see;
>   Where with my beautiful Fiammetta she
>   In God's most blissful presence taketh part.
>   Cino, Senuccio, Dante, thee around,
>   Gazing on things our reason may not grasp,
>   Calmly abide in sempiternal rest.
>   If here thy trusty friend I have been found,
>   Draw me to thee, that I may see and clasp
>   Her who love's flame first kindled in my breast.
>   *Francis Hueffer.*

Page 41.—Muratori in his treatise on the poetry of Italy bestows high praise on the sonnets of Lorenzo De' Medici, and of one of them he writes, "It is gold from the mine, mixed indeed with coarser materials, yet it is always gold." Lorenzo, surnamed the Magnificent, was born on 1st January 1448, and succeeded his father as the head of the republic of Florence at the age of twenty-three. His learning and delight in literature and art procured for him the name of the Augustus of Florence, and his influence, we are told, made that town the favoured seat of letters during his lifetime. "In a villa," writes Henry Hallam, "overhanging the towers of Florence, on the steep slope of that lofty hill crowned by the mother city, the ancient Fiesole, in gardens which Tully might have envied, with Ficino, Landino, and Politian at his side, he delighted his hours of leisure with the beautiful visions of Platonic philosophy, for which the summer stillness of an Italian sky appears the most congenial accompaniment." ... "The same curious spirit which led him to fill his garden at Careggi with exotic flowers of the East, the first instance of a botanical collection in Europe, had introduced a new animal from the same regions. Herds of buffaloes, since naturalised in Italy, whose dingy hide, bent neck, curved horns, and lowering aspect contrasted with the greyish hue and full, mild eye of the Tuscan oxen, pastured in the valley, down which the yellow Arno steals silently through its long reaches to the sea." This is a pleasant picture, and life, one thinks, were indeed well worth living under such favourable conditions.

A large portion of Lorenzo's poetry is religious, but the following sonnet is in his lighter strain. It is taken from the *London Magazine*, where the translator's name is not given:—

> "Oft on the recollection sweet I dwell,—
> Yea, never from my mind can aught efface
> The dress my mistress wore, the time, the place.
> Where first she fixed my eyes in raptured spell.
> How she then looked, thou, Love, remember'st well,
> For thou her side hast never ceased to grace ;
> Her gentle air, her meek, angelic face,
> The powers of language and of thought excel.
> When o'er the mountain-peaks deep-clad in snow
> Apollo pours a flood of golden light,
> So down her white-robed limbs did stream her hair :
> The time and place 't were words but lost to show ;
> It must be day, where shines a sun so bright,
> And Paradise where dwells a form so fair."

Lorenzo died in 1492, and the story of his life has been the subject of many biographers. In our own country William Roscoe published in the year 1800 an account of the life of Lorenzo in three volumes, from which are taken the three translations given at pages 41-43 of this selection.

Page 43.—Mr. Roscoe points out that Spenser (Lodowick Bryskett) has a passage similar to this sonnet in his *Mourning Muse of Thestylis*—

> "The blinded archer boy,
>   Like lark in shower of rain,
> Sat bathing of his wings,
>   And glad the time did spend
> Under those crystal drops
>   Which fell from her fair eyes,
> And at their brightest beams
>   Him proyn'd in lovely wise."

Warton in his observations on the "Fairy Queen" (vol. i. p. 223) has traced this passage to Ariosto—

> "Così a le belle lagrime le piume
> Si bagna amore, e gode al chiaro lume,"

though he thinks Spenser's verses bear a stronger resemblance to those of Nic. Archias (or the Count Nicolo d'Arco, a Latin poet of the 16th century):—

> "Tum suavi in pluvia nitens Cupido,
> Insidebat, uti solet volucris,
> Ramo, vere novo, ad novos tepores
> Post solem accipere ætheris liquores
> Gestire et pluviæ ore blandiendo."

Page 44.—This sonnet was attributed to Leonardo da Vinci in 1584 by Lomazzo, but it has since been attributed to various other authors, and Sig. G. Uzielli, in the journal *Il Buonarroti*, published in Rome, has recently affirmed that it must have been written some fifty years before the date of Leonardo. If such be really the case, it would be interesting to know how the sonnet came to be attributed to the great painter. If Leonardo had been a poet it would not have been surprising that he should have been accredited with a composition that did not belong to him, but as he was not, Lomazzo must, one would imagine, have had some reason for believing that the sonnet was his work.

But whether it was written by Leonardo or not, it is, we think, a very remarkable composition, and in this respect very different to the following mediocre sonnet by Raphael, which the latter has inscribed on one of his drawings now exhibited at the British Museum—

SONNET BY RAPHAEL.

Un pensier dolce erimembrare e godo
   Di quello assalto, ma più gravo el danno
   Del partir, ch' io restai como quei c' anno
In mar perso la stella, s' el ver odo.
Or lingua di parlar disogli el nodo
   A dir di questo inusitato inganno
   Ch' amor mi fece per mio grave afanno,
   Ma lui più ne ringratio, e lei ne lodo.
L'ora sesta era, che l' ocaso un sole
   Aveva fatto, e l' altro sur se in locho
   Ati più da far fati, che parole.
Ma io restai pur vinto al mio gran focho
   Che mi tormenta, che dove lon sole
   Desiar di parlar, più riman fiocho.

There are also two other sonnets attributed to Raphael, but they can hardly be considered worthy of his illustrious name.

Page 56.—I have included this sonnet in the selection, but not without considerable hesitation, because, although unquestionably a fine poem, there is little of it that can be said to really belong to Michael Angelo. His sonnets, as is well known, were not published until some fifty-nine years after his death, and were then given to the world in the year 1623 by his great-nephew, Michael Angelo Buonarroti the younger, with many additions and with numberless alterations of the original text. It is of this garbled version, this *rifacimento*, that Wordsworth has here given us a translation. Mr. J. A. Symonds, on the other hand, has followed the autograph of the sonnets first collated and published in 1863 by Signor Cesare Guasti.

It is interesting to note that the larger portion of Michael Angelo's sonnets were written during the period (1542-1547) of his intimacy with Vittoria Colonna; and Mr. Walter Pater justly observes—"It was because Vittoria raised no great passion that the space in his life where she reigns has such peculiar suavity; the spirit of the sonnets is lost if we once take them out of that dreamy atmosphere in which men have things as they will, because the hold of all outward things upon them is faint and thin. Their prevailing tone is a calm and meditative sweetness. The cry of distress is indeed there, but as a mere residue, a trace of bracing chalybeate salt, just discernible in the song, which rises as a clear, sweet spring from a charmed space in his life."—(*The Renaissance*, p. 91.)

Of all the Italian sonnets there are none of greater worth, none of higher tone or nobility of thought and feeling, than are those of Michael Angelo. Where, for instance, shall we find one more pure, more perfect, more sublime, than that on *Celestial Love*, which Mr. Symonds has so excellently translated ; or that on *Love's Justification*, which Wordsworth has immortalised? These, as also that entitled *A Prayer for Purification*, stand forth pre-eminent as the work of a man who has learned to think clearly, and feel deeply, and is well acquainted with the innermost recesses of the human heart.

The following is Wordsworth's rendering of the sonnet given at page 50 :—

"No mortal object did these eyes behold
When first they met the placid light of thine,
And my soul felt her destiny divine,
And hope of endless peace in me grew bold:
Heaven-born, the soul a heav'nward course must hold;
Beyond the visible world she soars to seek
(For what delights the sense is false and weak)
Ideal form, the universal mould.
The wise man, I affirm, can find no rest
In that which perishes; nor will he lend
His heart to ought which doth on time depend.
'Tis sense, unbridled will, and not true love,
Which kills the soul: Love betters what is best,
Even here below, but more in heaven above."

This is, we think, inferior to Mr. Symonds's translation, but the termination of the sonnet in the above rendering is well expressed, and worthy of Wordsworth's poetic genius.

Page 58.—The following extracts from Vasari's "Lives of the Painters" respecting Cardinal Bembo are not without interest:—

"Among the portraits executed by Giovanni Bellini was that of a lady beloved by Messer Pietro Bembo, before the latter went to Rome to Pope Leo X.; and whom he portrayed with so much truth and animation, that as Simon of Siena was celebrated by the first Petrarch the Florentine; so was Giovanni by this second Petrarch the Venetian, as may be seen in the sonnet,

'O imagine mia celeste e pura,'

wherein he says, in the commencement of the second quatrain,

'Credo che 'l mio Bellin con la figura,'

with that which follows. And what greater reward could our artists desire for their labours than that of seeing

themselves celebrated by the pens of illustrious poets, as the
most excellent Titian, also by the learned Messer Giovanni
della Casa, in that sonnet which begins—

'Ben veggo io Tiziano, in forme nuove.'"

. . . . .

"He who knows how closely, not only painting, but all
the arts of design resemble poetry, knows also that verse
proceeding from the poetic *furor* is the only good and true
poesy: in like manner the works of men excellent in the
arts of design are much better when produced by the force
of a sudden inspiration, than when they are the result of
long beating about, and gradual spinning forth with pains
and labour. Whoever has the clear idea of what he desires
to produce in his mind, as all ought to have from the first
instant, will ever march confidently and with readiness
towards the perfection of the work which he proposes to
execute. Nevertheless, as all minds are not of the same
character, there are, doubtless, some who can only do well
when they proceed slowly, but the instances are rare. And,
not to confine ourselves to painting, there is a proof of this
among poets, as we are told, in the practice of the most
venerable and most learned Bembo, who laboured in such
sort that he would sometimes expend many months, nay,
possibly years, if we dare give credit to the words of those
who affirm it, in the production of a sonnet."

Page 66.—Erasmi Di Valvasone was born about the
year 1523, and was the author of the *Angeleida*, which
Hayley and Warton affirmed that Milton had copied in
certain passages of his *Paradise Lost*. I would here
mention that James Glassford, whose excellent transla-
tions of this and several other sonnets are given in this
volume, was born at Dougalston, in Scotland, at the
close of the last century. Some of his translations first
appeared in the *London Magazine* in 1823, and were
afterwards collected together and published under the

R*

title of *Lyrical Compositions from the Italian Poets* in 1834. A writer in the *Edinburgh Review* observes respecting them—"We have been greatly pleased with this little volume, as much from its general character as from the grace and polish of its execution. It is evidently the production of one possessing a quick natural sensibility to natural beauty, improved by art and study, and no inattentive observer of the poetry of our times."

Page 76.—Giovanni Domenico Campanella was born in the year 1568 at Stilo, in Calabria. "His keen interest in philosophy," writes Mr. J. A. Symonds, "and his admiration for the great Dominican doctors, Thomas Aquinas and Albertus Magnus, induced him, at the age of fifteen, to enter the Order of St. Dominic, exchanging his secular name for Tommaso. But the old alliance between philosophy and orthodoxy, drawn up by scholasticism and approved by the mediæval church, had been succeeded by mutual hostility; and the youthful thinker found no favour in the cloister of Cosenza, where he now resided. The new philosophy taught by Telesio placed itself in direct antagonism to the pseudo-Aristotelian tenets of the theologians, and founded its own principles upon the Interrogation of Nature. Telesio, says Bacon, was the prince of the *novi homines*, or inaugurators of modern thought. It was natural that Campanella should be drawn towards this great man." And the result was that he became "an object of suspicion to his brethren, . . . his papers were seized at Bologna; and at Rome the Holy Inquisition condemned him to perpetual incarceration, on the ground that he derived his science from the devil, that he had written the book, *De tribus Impostoribus*, that he was a follower of Democritus, and that his opposition to Aristotle savoured of gross heresy. . . . Though nothing was proved against him, Campanella was held a prisoner under the sentence which the Inquisition had pronounced upon him. For twenty-five years he remained in Neapolitan dungeons; three times during that period he was tortured to the verge of dying; and at last he was released, while quite an old man, at the urgent request of the French Court. Not many years after his liberation Campanella died."

His sonnets are remarkable for their depth of thought and clearness of vision, although they are by no means free from the prevailing errors of the age in which he lived. Truth and Nature, the handmaidens of philosophy, mainly formed the subject of his verse; and as he indicates in his sonnet "To the Poets," he preferred "sound sense to idle lays," "beauty to paint and dress." In his own words—

"That tale alone is worth the pondering
Which hath not smothered history in lies,
And arms the soul against each sinful thing."

Page 87.—This sonnet by Lodovico Paterno is a paraphrase from the Latin of Navagero :—

" Auræ quæ levibus percurritis aëra pennis,
Et strepitis blando per nemora alta sono ;
Serta dat hæc vobis, vobis hæc rusticus Idmon
Spargit odorato plena canistra croco.
Vos lenite æstum, et paleas sejungite inanes,
Dum medio fruges ventilat ille die."

Which lines have also been imitated by the French poet, Joachim du Bellay, in his *D'un Vanneur de blé aux vents* :—

" A vous trouppe legere
Qui d'aile passagere
Par le monde volez,

> Et d'un sifflant murmure
> L' ombrageuse verdure
> Doucement esbranlez
> J' offre ces violettes,
> Ces lis et ces fleurettes,
> Et ces roses icy
> Ces vermeillettes roses,
> Tout freschement éclauses,
> Et ces œillets aussi.
> De vostre douce haleine
> Evantez ceste pleine,
> Evantez ce sejour :
> Cependant que j' ahanne
> A mon blé, que je vanne
> A la chaleur du jour."

For an excellent translation of these lines see Mr. Lang's *Ballads and Lyrics of Old France*.

Page 93.—I find this translation in the notes to Longfellow's translation of Dante's *Paradiso*. . . . The sonnets of Filicaja have somewhat of a Miltonic grandeur in their soul-animating strains, and the one, so often referred to, addressed to Italy (page 97), might well have been written by Wordsworth. It is incorporated by Lord Byron in his *Childe Harold*, (canto iv.) in the following stanzas :—

> "Italia ! oh Italia ! thou who hast
> The fatal gift of beauty, which became
> A funeral dower of present woes and past,
> On thy sweet brow is sorrow ploughed by shame
> And annals graved in characters of flame,
> Oh, God ! that thou wert in thy nakedness
> Less lovely and more powerful, and couldst claim
> Thy right, and awe the robbers back, who press
> To shed thy blood, and drink the tears of thy distress ;

>   Then might'st thou more appal ; or, less desired,
>   Be homely and be peaceful, undeplored
>   For thy destructive charms ; then, still untired,
>   Would not be seen the armëd torrents poured
>   Down the deep Alps ; nor would the hostile horde
>   Of many-nationed spoilers from the Po
>   Quaff blood and water ; nor the stranger's sword
>   Be thy sad weapon of defence, and so,
> Victor or vanquished, thou the slave of friend or foe."

"There is, indeed," writes Sismondi, "only one Italian poet belonging to the seventeenth century distinguished for his patriotic sentiments. That poet is the senator Filicaja. It is somewhat remarkable with what ardour the spark of ancient liberty revived in his breast. He was a Florentine, born on the thirtieth of December 1642, and he closed his career on the twenty-fifth of September 1707. His genius took its source in deep national and religious feelings, and in interests affecting the repose of Europe. It was first excited by witnessing the siege of Vienna by the Turks, in the year 1683, and its gallant defence by Charles V., Duke of Lorraine, with its final deliverance by John Sobieski. Filicaja composed several *canzoni*, breathing heroic ardour, joy, and religious gratitude, in celebration of the Christian victory, and in a style very superior to anything we find in the works of other poets of the age. . . . One of his sonnets (see page 97) maintains, to this day, the highest degree of reputation ; and it is, perhaps, the most celebrated poetic specimen which the Italian literature of the seventeenth century affords."—(*Lit. of the South of Europe*, vol. ii.)

Page 100.—A writer in the *Edinburgh Review* for October 1804 observes,—" Were we called upon to give a decided preference to any one sonnet in the Italian language, we should certainly be inclined to say that the sonnet of Gaetana Passerini, commencing, *Genova mia, se con asciutto ciglio* (Mathias, vol. iii. p. 331), is superior to any in Petrarch. We imagine it was written after the bombardment of Genoa, by Louis the Fourteenth, in 1684. Mr. Mathias is mistaken in saying that Passerini died in 1714. She was living in 1726, when Bergalli published her *Rimatrici d'ogni secolo*. Her works, we believe, have never been collected, but are scattered in different *Scelte* and in the *Rime degli Arcadi*. We have seen little more than twenty of her sonnets and anacreontic odes; but the specimen of her poetry given by Mr. Mathias ought not to have stood alone. The sonnet addressed to Prince Eugene, *Signor, che nella destra*, and several others, have considerable merit."

Page 111.—This sonnet relates to Pope Gregory XVI., who, it will be remembered, was highly obnoxious to the progressive party in Italy, as being a stolid upholder of the old regime, or, as Rossetti here calls it, the *Status quo*. Mr. William Michael Rossetti, in forwarding me the translation, observes, "The sonnet has a point of oddity, or comicality, in its form which cannot be exhibited (though it is literally reproduced) in the English translation. While Italian sonnets usually have eleven syllables in each line ending with a dissyllabic rhyme, this by my father has only ten, like an English sonnet, so that every line ends with a strong accentuated emphasis. This is what Italians call 'versi tronchi,' and would not be used unless with a grotesque intention."

Gabriele Rossetti, the illustrious father of an illustrious family, was born in 1783, at Vasto, a small Italian town situated in the hilly district of the Abruzzi. The principal piazza of this little place already bears his name, and a statue to his memory is, we believe, to be erected therein. He was a poet of considerable reputation in his own country, and he was also a patriot, and the unfortunate result of his endeavouring, with other patriotic Neapolitans, to obtain a satisfactory constitution from King Ferdinand, was, that he had to escape from his native land in order to save his life. Lady Moore, the wife of the Admiral in command of the English fleet stationed in the Bay of Naples, being an admirer of the poems and character of Rossetti, persuaded her husband and another officer to go ashore and rescue the poet, whom they succeeded in carrying off in disguise, and conveyed to Malta. After four years' residence in that island, Rossetti came to live in London, where he married Frances Polidori, sister to Dr. Polidori who travelled with Lord Byron, and daughter of Signor Polidori, secretary to Alfieri. He died in the year 1854.

Page 116.—Pierre Ronsard was born in 1524, at the Château de la Poissonnière, in the province of Vendôme, and at the age of nine was sent to the Collége de Navarre at Paris. He was afterwards removed by his father to Avignon, and placed in the service of Francis, the eldest son of the French king, and subsequently in that of James V. of Scotland. An illness which produced total deafness caused him to withdraw from public life and devote himself to literary pursuits, in which he soon became illustrious, and was judged by Francis the First to be a greater poet than Mellin de Saint-Gelais.

Very various, however, have been the opinions and judgments of critics respecting him; and while Pasquier declared that Rome never produced a greater poet than

Ronsard, Boileau sarcastically observed that "his Muse in French spoke Greek and Latin." "His epic, the Franciade," writes Mr. Andrew Lang, "is as tedious as other artificial epics, and his odes are almost unreadable. We are never allowed to forget that he is the poet who read the 'Iliad' through in three days. He is, as has been said of Le Brun, more mythological than Pindar. His constant allusion to his grey hair, an affectation which may be noticed in Shelley, is borrowed from Anacreon. Many of the sonnets in which he 'petrarquizes,' retain the faded odour of the roses he loved; and his songs have fire and melancholy and a sense as of perfume from 'a closet long to quiet vowed, with mothed and dropping arras hung.' Ronsard's great fame declined when Malherbe came to 'bind the sweet influences of the Pleiad,' but he has been duly honoured by the newest school of French poetry."

Pedantry and affectation were his faults, and the faults of the age in which he lived; and it has been said that he displayed so much erudition in his verses, that his mistresses, in order to understand them, had to resort to the very dangerous aid of *foreign commentators*. Yet, all this notwithstanding, his sonnets have a pathos, elegance, and delicate fragrance, and one is not astonished to be told that his verse consoled the unhappy Mary Stuart in her imprisonment, and that she presented to him a silver Parnassus, inscribed with the words,—

"*À Ronsard, l'Apollon de la source des Muses.*"

We may, however, be surprised to learn that Queen Elizabeth was also one of his admirers, and compared him to a valuable diamond, of which she made him a present.

As a writer of sonnets there are few among the French

poets who are at all comparable with Ronsard, and to the translations which are given in our selection the following by the poet, John Keats, should be added. It may be mentioned that the last two lines are by Lord Houghton, and that the translation, as originally written by Keats, ended at the twelfth line. It is taken from the *Life, Letters, and Literary Remains*, edited by Lord Houghton, and is included by Keats in a letter to his friend, Reynolds :—

" Nature withheld Cassandra in the skies,
  For more adornment, a full thousand years ;
  She took their cream of Beauty's fairest dies,
  And shaped and tinted her above all Peers :
  Meanwhile Love kept her dearly with his wings,
  And underneath their shadow fill'd her eyes
  With such a richness that the cloudy Kings
  Of high Olympus utter'd slavish sighs.
  When from the Heavens I saw her first descend,
  My heart took fire, and only burning pains—
  They were my pleasures—they my Life's sad end ;
  Love pour'd her beauty into my warm veins,
  [So that her image in my soul upgrew,
  The only thing adorable and true]."

Page 128.—Joachim du Bellay—who was called by his contemporaries the French Ovid—was a kinsman of the Cardinal Du Bellay, and was born about the year 1525. Mr. Lang writes—"There is something in Du Bellay's life, in the artistic nature checked by occupation in affairs—he was the secretary of Cardinal Du Bellay—in the regret and affection with which Rome depressed and allured him, which reminds the English reader of the thwarted career of Clough." In his sonnet on "Venice" there is, indeed, a strange resemblance to the manner and method, the keen sparkling satire and graphic

representation, which characterise so much of Clough's
poetry. His sonnet, "To Courtiers," might also be
mentioned as an example of his light yet caustic
humour. His poetry was very highly esteemed by
Edmund Spenser, who not only translated a number of
his sonnets, but also annexed thereto some highly
laudatory lines:—

" Bellay! first garland of free poesy
　That France brought forth, though fruitful of brave
　　　wits,
　Well worthy thou of immortality."

Page 138.—Cary, in his volume on the *Early French
Poets*, writes:—"It is entertaining enough, after read-
ing the poems of Ronsard, to look into those of Amadis
Jamyn, his page, who has quite as much of the airs of
his master as one in that station ought to have. In
imitation of his master, he has three mistresses, after
whom he names three of his books (there are five books
in all)—Oriana, christened after the mistress of Amadis
of Gaul; Artemis; and Callirhoe. Like Ronsard, he
pays his compliments in verse to the French monarchs,
Charles IX. and Henry III., the former of whom, I
believe, appointed him his secretary." It is a mistake,
however, on the part of Cary to speak of Jamyn as being
the page of Ronsard. The latter, delighted with Jamyn's
verses, invited him to his house, and, we are told, treated
him as his own son, and eventually procured for him the
post of Secretary and Reader to the King.

Page 143.—Francois de la Mothe le Vayer, member of
the French Academy and preceptor of Louis XIV., lost
his son in 1664, and Molière, in forwarding him this
sonnet, observes,—" Vous voyez bien, Monsieur, que

je m' écarte fort du chemin qu'on suit d'ordinaire en pareille rencontre, que le Sonnet que je vous envoye n'est rien moins qu' une consolation ; mais j'ay crû qu' il falloit en user de la sorte avec vous, & que c'est consoler un Philosophe que de luy justifier ses larmes, & de mettre sa douleur en liberté. Si je n'ay pas trouvé d'assez fortes raisons pour affranchir vostre tendresse des severes lecons de la Philosophie, & pour vous obliger á pleurer sans contrainte, il en faut accuser le peu d'éloquence d'un homme qui ne scauroit persuader ce qu' il sçait si bien faire."

Page 164.—Mr. Straug, in his "Germany in 1831," observes, respecting the mausoleum of the late queen of Prussia—"There is no inscription on the marble, or on the mausoleum. Queen Louisa required none. The virtues of her life, and the causes of her early death, are not only well known, but deeply engraven on the memory of the Prussian people. The being who perished of a broken heart, for the wrongs inflicted by a foreign foe upon her people, and who dropped into an untimely tomb, the victim of lacerated patriotism, is indeed worthy to be the idol of a nation's memory. . . . . During the liberation-war, the name of Louisa became a watchword in favour of national independence, while her patriotism proved a tutelar genius to the Prussian army."

Page 189.—This sonnet by Cervantes, in honour of the City of Rome, is said to have been the last sonnet that he wrote. It is to be found in his *Persiles and Sigismunda*, and is followed by these words: "When the pilgrim had finished reciting this sonnet, he turned to the bystanders and said, 'A few years ago there came to his holy city a Spanish poet, a mortal enemy

to himself and a disgrace to his nation, who made
and composed a sonnet, reviling this illustrious city and
its noble inhabitants ; but his throat will pay the fault
of his tongue, should they catch him. I, not as a poet,
but as a Christian, as if to make amends for his crime,
composed what you have heard !' "

More curious, however, and worthy of the genius
of Cervantes, is that entitled, *The Author to His Pen*,
which forms the frontispiece of his *Journey to
Parnassus*. The following quaint prologue to that
work is also admirable:—"If haply, curious reader,
thou art a poet, and this *Journey* should come (be
it even stealthiwise) into thy hands, and thou find
thyself inscribed therein and noted as one of the good
poets, give thanks to Apollo for the grace he hath
given thee ; and if thou do not so find thyself, in
like manner mayst thou give thanks. And God be
with thee."

Page 195.—This somewhat celebrated sonnet is taken
from Lope de Vega's *Nina de Plata*. It has been translated by Edwards, author of the *Canons of Criticism*, and
others; but the late Mr. Gibson's rendering is the most successful in depicting the dexterous ease and rapidity with
which the poet overcomes the difficulties of the form.
It is, perhaps, not generally known that the credit of
the idea of the *Soneto del Soneto* belongs to Diego Hurtado
de Mendoza, who flourished some fifty years before Lope
de Vega. The sonnets of both of them are placed side
by side in the *Parnaso Español*, tom. iv. 22, 23. These
sonnets have been translated or imitated in various other
languages—as, for instance, in Italian by Marino, and in
French by Voiture and Desmarais. Lord Holland, in
his *Life of Lope de Vega*, states that the sonnet seems
to have been his favourite employment, and that there

are few of his plays which do not contain three or four
of these little poems.

Page 196.—This sonnet, by Lupercio Leonardo, is taken
from the Notes of the late Mr. Gibson's translation of
the *Journey to Parnassus*, by Cervantes. Lupercio was
born at Barbastro, in Aragon, in the year 1564 ; and he
and his brother, Bartolomé Juan Leonardo, were styled
the *Horaces* of Spain, "on account of their classical
refinement and the exquisite character of their satires."

Page 220.—I know not how it may seem to others,
but to me this sonnet, by Boccage, on "Nelson,"
appears to possess unusual merit, and Mr. J. J. Aubertin
has given us a very admirable rendering. The two
opening lines of the sestet—

> " Incarnadined with blood I left the wave,
> A bolt upon the furious Gaul I threw "—

are excellent, as also are the lines which close the
sonnet—

> " He to whom Victory vast regions gave
> Envies the man who did one race subdue."

The author, Manoel Maria de Barbosa du Boccage, was
born at Setubal in the year 1766. After his education
was finished he obtained a commission in the infantry
of Setubal, but subsequently entered the naval service.
He is said to have acquired a high reputation as an
improvisatore, and as a poet he appears to have been
especially remarkable for his powers of satire. After an
absence of five years in India, during which time he lost
the manuscript of the first volume of his works through
shipwreck, he returned to Lisbon, and was well received.

Unfortunately, he afterwards became associated with
dissolute company, and was ordered to be imprisoned by
the Inquisition. The Marquesses of Ponte de Lima and
of Abrantes obtained his release, but he soon returned
to his old habits, and died at the age of thirty-nine in
the year 1805.

Some bald translations of his sonnets will be found in
Adamson's *Lusitania Illustrata*, published at Newcastle-
on-Tyne in 1842.

Page 223.—The following particulars respecting the
Swedish poets are given me by Mr. Gosse :—The sonnet·
was introduced into Sweden by Gustaf Rosenhane, who
wrote a hundred sonnets, under the general title of
Venerid, in 1648. He was at this time in his thirtieth
year, having been born in 1619. Rosenhane, who was
of good family, was made a baron in 1654, and attained
high honours in the state before his death in 1684.
With Stjernhjelm, he divides the honour of having
created modern Swedish poetry, and though artificial,
he is a writer of very considerable merit. His sonnets
were inspired, not by Petrarch, but by Ronsard. In a
somewhat pedantic preface to his *Venerid*, he confesses
that he was incited to become a sonneteer, not so much
by passion, as by a wish to enrich and improve the
stubborn soil of the Swedish language. Rosenhane
remained for several years the only Swedish sonneteer.

Olof Wexionius was born in Dorpat in 1656, and was
taken to Abo in Finland as an infant, when the Russians
drove the Swedes out of Livonia in 1658. Very little is
known of his career, which closed prematurely in 1690,
while he was acting as a secretary in Sweden. He
published a small volume of poems, now excessively
scarce in 1864 ; there exists a MS. list of his additional
writings, including a great many sonnets, none of which

appear to have survived him. The sonnet here translated was written on the occasion of the funeral of a noble and pious lady, the Countess Catharina Rosenfeldt, in Upsala Cathedral, in September 1689, and it is therefore probably the latest of the poems of Wexionius.

Page 231.—Dr. Garnett has furnished me with the following facts respecting the life and history of the author of these sonnets :—Adam Mickiewicz, the greatest of Polish poets, was born at the village of Zaosie, near Nowogrodek, on December 24, 1798, and was the second son of an advocate descended from an ancient Lithuanian family. His first poems of importance, breathing the spirit of the romantic school, were published in 1822 and 1823, and includes the first part of his "Dziady, or Feast of the Dead," which became well known in Western Europe through an essay by George Sand. His metrical romance, "Grazyna," followed. In 1825 a visit to the Crimea inspired his Crimean sonnets, and in 1828 appeared his epic of "Konrad Wallenrod." He had now become exceedingly popular, but an unhappy attachment drove him from his country, and the insurrection of 1831, with which he warmly sympathised, prevented his return. He continued his "Dziady" in a highly mystical style, and in 1834 produced his masterpiece, "Master Thadeus," the national epic of his country. Nothing can show greater versatility of talent than the contrast between the wild fancy of his other epics and the clear, objective character-painting and dramatic humour of this picture of Lithuanian life at the beginning of the century. From this time Mickiewicz wrote little more poetry. He became professor of Slavonic at the College de France, where a great career seemed before him, but unfortunately fell under the influence of a mystical enthusiast named Towianski, and his lectures had to be suppressed. Louis Napoleon made him librarian of the Arsenal, which post he resigned on the outbreak of the Crimean War, and proceeded to Constantinople to organise a Polish legion. He died there on 28th November 1855: his remains were brought back to France and interred at Montmorency. His "Konrad Wallenrod" and "Master Thadeus" have been admirably translated into English by Miss Maude Ashurst Briggs.

Page 235.—Mrs. Edmonds, who resided for some time in Greece, and is thoroughly conversant with the poetry of that country, has kindly supplied me with the following particulars respecting modern Greek sonnets:—
"The Sonnet may be said to have only just found its way into Hellenic poetry, and the examples met with among the compositions of the poets of the Athenian school, or of those who have studied in foreign universities, are as yet but few in number. In the large selection from seventy-nine poets of this century comprised in *Parnassos*,* which covers 1040 pages, close type, there are two sonnets only, by Antonios Manousos, which, although good in construction, are of small value. Among the graceful lyrics of George Drosinês there is but one sonnet, which is of distinct inferiority. George Viziênos, so successful in his charming legendary poems, fails here; and in the fourteen sonnets contained in his last volume, Αἱ Ἀτθίδες Αὐραι† there is the radical defect of the use of Alexandrines, as well as a want of freshness and spontaneity. The reason of this tardy use of the sonnet among the prolific poets of New Hellas

* Collected and edited by "Mataranghas." Athens, 1881.
† Trübner & Co., 1883.

may, perhaps, be ascribed to the strong hold which the
national poetry still retains on the affections of every
patriotic Greek. The influence of the orally transmitted
poetry of the people seems ever to be in like measure
with the gift of genius. In proof of this, the names of
Aristotle Valaôritês, and Julius Typaldos need only be
cited from among many others. The part that the
singers played in keeping alive the fire of freedom, and
in rekindling its flames from the expiring ashes, is well
known. From Klephtic songs to Rhegas—to Kalvos,
Solomos, Zalokostas, and the Soutzos, the voice was
never silent; and with them, as with living writers, a
greater charm seems to cling to national themes written
in the language of the people. For the sonnet, however,
the vernacular forms are wholly unsuited.

"Respecting the authors of the two sonnets trans-
lated, it may be stated that the reputation of Alex. R.
Rhangabe, as a writer of great intellectual activity, is
known almost throughout Europe. Born in 1810, of an
aristocratic Phanariote family, he inherited from his
father, James Rhizos-Rhangabe, his talent for letters,
which has been displayed in nearly every branch of
literature. His studies were completed in Germany, in
which country he has long resided. His eleven volumes
of collected works, Tὰ ʼΑπαντά, contain eight sonnets.

"Aristomenês Provilegios was born in the Island of
Sephnos in 1850, and studied philosophy at Athens,
Munich, Leipzig, and Jena. He has long been a con-
tributor to the high-class Athenian weekly periodical,
Hestia, has written a long poem on the "Apple of Dis-
cord," and has lately been engaged on a translation of
"Faust," and also upon a volume of Odes and Lyrics.
His style, if not forcible, is refined, and his language
well chosen."

The following is the original of the sonnet on "Love,"

by Alex. R. Rhangabe, the translation of which is given at page 236:—

Ὁ Ἔρως

Ἰδὲ, ὦ φίλη μου, τὸ πᾶν διασκοσμῶν ὁ πλάσας,
Τὴν γῆν μας κατεσκέυασεν ἀπὸ δακρύων ζύμην,
Εἰς δάκρυα τὴν ἡδονὴν, εἰς δάκρυα τὴν φήμην,
Εἰς δάκρυα συνέμιξε τὰς ἀπολαύσεις πάσας.

Περᾷ μ'ἀγῶνας ὁ Θνητὸς ἠπείρους καὶ Θαλάσσας·
περᾷ καὶ δὲν κατέλιπεν οὐδ' ἴχνος οὐδὲ μνήμην.
Δακρύων πρὸς τὴν ἄναυδον προστρέχει ἐπιστήμην,
Καὶ πρὶν σπουδάσῃ τὴν ζωὴν, ἀπέθανε γηράσας.

Οἱ πόθοι του ἀμφίβολοι εἰς μαῦρον πλέουν χάος.
Ἐλπίζει, κ'αἱ ἐλπίδες του μαραίνονται ἀκαίρως.
Σκιὰς διώκει πτερωτὰς, πλὴν φεύγουν ἀεννάως.

Ἑνὸς δὲ μόνου πρὸς αὐτὸν εἰρηνικοῦ ἀστέρος,
Ἕρπει ἀκτὶς ἐλλάμπουσα διὰ τοῦ σκότους πρᾴως,
Ἓν μόνον τὸν παραμυθεῖ μειδίαμα,—ὁ Ἔρως.

Page 240.—Pieter Corneliszoon Hooft (1581-1647), the celebrated Dutch poet and historian, whose Castle of Muidea was for nearly forty years the centre of literary and artistic activity in Holland, was the earliest Dutch sonnet-writer. He first imitated Petrarch, and introduced Italian poetry to the attention of his countrymen, after his famous journey to the south of Europe in 1599. Vondel, the greatest of Dutch poets, wrote a few sonnets,

NOTES. 275

but they are harsh and tuneless compositions. The sonnet has been almost, if not entirely, unattempted in recent Dutch literature.

Page 242.—This unique Latin sonnet by Hugo Grotius is printed at the beginning of Thomas Farnabie's edition of the "Tragedies of Seneca," published at Leyden and London in 1624. The following is an exact copy of the original:—"Literatissimo, amicissimo, candidissimoque pectori, Thomæ Farnabio, sonulum hendeca-syllabicum sacro."

> Vitæ Scena magistra singularis,
>   Scenæ vita Tragædus; in tragædis
>   Lux primæ Seneca est suprema sedis;
>   Quâ TV lux Senecæ simul locaris.
> Das Stellis supereminere claris,
>   Tanquam ardentibus undecunque tedis,
>   Et mendis Tragici medere fœdis;
>   Nostris unde nepotibus canaris.
> Lugdunum néq: te modò Batavis,
>   Londinumve suis legat Britannis,
>   Urbem Æternus utram tenere mavis:
> Cunctis quin legitor locis & annis;
>   Nec linguis hominum ferire pravis,
>   Et cedat tibi temporum tyrannis.
>   *Hugo Hollandius.*

Thomas Farnabie was born in London in 1575, and is said by Anthony à Wood to have been "the chief grammarian, rhetorician, poet, and latinist of his time." (Athen: Oxon:) He edited Juvenal, Persius, Seneca, Martial, Ovid, Terence, and Lucian,—the *stellæ claræ* referred to in the fifth line of the sonnet.—He also wrote the Latin poem in the volume of *in memoriam* verse published on the death of Edward King, in which Milton's *Lycidas* first appeared.

Hugo Grotius (Huig de Groot) was born at Delft in 1583, and is renowned as being the most illustrious scholar of his age. He is one of the poets whom Milton has been accused of copying, and as Milton was introduced to him at Paris by Lord Scudamore, it is not improbable that Hugo Grotius' poem (*Adamus Exul*) was well known to our English poet when he wrote *Paradise Lost*. The similarity between the two poems, however, is not very striking, although the following excerpt from *Adamus Exul*, translated by F. Barham, is perhaps suggestive of "a Miltonic aggregation of vague geographical names,"—

> "Here the o'erflowing Phison issues forth,
> Araxes' royal tide, which clothes with green
> The Colchian plains, and clasps with strong embrace
> Havilah, and the Caspian land of gold,
> Bdellium and onyx. Towards the southern shore,
> Flows Gihon, or Choaspes, down the vales
> Of Persian Susiana. By his side
> Hiddekel ; the swift Tigris rolls his waves ;
> And furthest west, the broad Euphrates spreads
> His giant arms invincible, and fills
> Chaldea with his richness."

It may be mentioned that *Paradise Lost* was published in 1667, Andreini's *Adam* in 1613, and *Adamus Exul*, by Grotius, in 1601. Andreini's poem, it will be remembered, was said by Voltaire to have been the source of Milton's inspiration ; but the legend of Eden was manifestly a favourite subject with the poets of those days, for as early as 1593 William Hunnis, the author of *A Handful of Honeysuckles*, had published his poem entitled "Adam's Banishment," and it is quite unnecessary to mention the names of Vondel and Du Bartas.

INDEX TO AUTHORS.

	PAGE		PAGE
Aldana, F. De	217, 218	Cervantes	186-189
Ariosto	57	Chamisso	165
Arvers, F.	144, 145	Chiabrera, G.	74
Baudelaire	148-150	Cino da Pistoia	20
Bembo,	58, 59	Coppetta, F.	62
Bettinelli	110	Cotta, G.	99
Boccaccio	40 (Notes, p. 250).	Crescimbeni	98
Boccage	220	Dante 7-19 (Notes p. 247).	
Bonaggiunta	6	Desportes, P.	139, 140
Bondi, Clementi	105	Du Bellay	128-133
Broekhuizen, J. van.	241	Figueroa, F. de	182
Bruno, Giordano	75	Filicaja	93-97
Bürger, G. A.	157	Folgore da San Gemignano	21, 22
Burguillos, Tome	180		
Bussi, Giulio	86	Glatigny, A.	146
Calderon	197	Gleim, J. W. L.	166
Camoens	201-214	Goethe	158, 159
Campanella, T.	76-83	Grotius, Hugo	242
Casa, G. della	65	Guido Cavalcanti	3-5
Casti	106, 107	Guido Guinicelli	2

INDEX TO AUTHORS.

	PAGE		PAGE
Guittone d'Arezzo	1	Prudhomme, Sully	151-154
Heine	171-175	Quevedo	184
Hooft, P. C.	230, 240	Raphael (Notes, p. 254).	
Jamyn, Amadis	138	Rhangabe, A. R.	236
Jodelle, Estienne	137	Redi, F.	88-92
Körner, Theo.	164	Ronsard 116-127(Notes, p. 265).	
Labé, Louise	136	Rosenhane	223, 224
Leca, M. V. de	181	Rossetti, G.	111
Leonardo da Vinci	44	Salvator Rosa	84
Lobo, Rod.	216	Sanazzaro	45
Lope de Vega	191-195	Santa Teresa	183
Lorenzo de' Medici	41-43	Scarron, P.	142
Lupercio, Leonardo	196	Semedo, Curvo	219
Maldonado, L.	190	Stagnelius	226-228
Maratti, F.	104	Tahureau, J.	134, 135
Marini, G. B.	72, 73	Tarsis, Juan de	185
Matos, Xavier de	215	Tasso, B.	64
Mellin de Saint-Gelais	115	Tasso, T.	67-71
Metastasio	103	Tiedge	160-163
Michael Angelo	46-56	Tolomei	63
Mickiewicz	231, 232	Truffier	147
Molière	143	Uhland	168-170
Passerini, Gaetana	100	Valvasone, E. di	66
Pastorini	108	Viau, Theo. de	141
Paterno, L.	87	Vittoria Colonna	60, 61
Petrarch	23-39	Vittorelli	109
Petrocchi	85	Wexionius, O.	225
Platen-Hallermünde	167	Zappi	101, 102
Provilegios, Aristomenês	235		

INDEX TO TRANSLATORS.

	PAGE
Ashe, Thomas	126, 127, 144
Aubertin, J. J.	201-212, 220
Bowring, E. A.	158, 175
Bowring, Sir J.	179-181, 183
Brooks, C. T.	160-164
Bryant	219
Byron, Lord	109
Cary,	1, 2, 5, 8, 9, 17, 18, 87, 118, 137-139
Cayley, C. B.	6, 34-39
Dacre, Lady	31, 32
De Vere, Sir A.	74, 86, 102
Dickson, M.	168, 171, 173
Dobson, Austin	115, 130, 131, 143
Edmonds, E. M.	235, 236
Garnett, R.	214-216, 231, 232
Gibson, J. Y.	186, 189, 195, 196
Gilsa, Baroness von	70, 72
Glassford, J.	45, 57-62, 64, 66, 67, 69, 73, 85, 96, 98-100, 103, 105
Gosse, Edmund	88-92, 141, 223-228, 239, 240
Gray, F. C.	40
Hemans, Felicia	184, 185
Herbert, Hon. W.	182
Higginson, Colonel	25-30
Holland, Lord	194
Hoole, John	71
Hueffer, F. (Notes, p. 250).	
Hunt, Leigh	93, 106-108
Jarvis, C.	187, 188
Keats (Notes, p. 265).	
Lang, Andrew	120, 121, 123-125, 132-135, 146, 147
Le Mesurier, T.	94, 95, 101
Lofft, Capel	157
Longfellow,	145, 190-192, 217, 218

INDEX TO TRANSLATORS.

	PAGE
Lowell, James Russell	19
Lytton, Earl of	116, 117
Martin, Sir Theodore	11-13
Merivale, J. Horman	. 68
Monkhouse, Cosmo	119, 150
Montgomery, James	. 110
Norton, C. E.	15, 16
O'Shaughnessy, A.	151-154
Ossoli, M. Fuller	. 159
Parsons, Dr.	. 14
Paul, Kegan	122 (Notes p. 247).
Pike, Warburton	4, 10, 20
Platt, Alexander	169, 170
Platt, Arthur	136, 197
Ropes, A. R.	148, 149
Roscoe, William	41, 42, 43
Rossetti, D. G. (Notes, p. 246).	
Rossetti, W. M.	84, 111
Russell, Thomas	33, 104, 166
Shelley	3, 7
Southey	213
Spenser	128, 129
Stratheir	172, 174
Surrey, Earl of	23
Symonds, J. A.	21, 22, 46-54, 65, 75-83
Tomlinson, C.	193
Waddington, S.	44, 140, 241 (Notes, p. 247).
Wordsworth	55, 56 (Notes, p. 256).
Wyatt, Sir Thomas	24

www.ingramcontent.com/pod-product-compliance
Lightning Source LLC
Chambersburg PA
CBHW030816230426
43667CB00008B/1240